LEGO DC UNIVERSE™ SUPER HEROES

BATMAN™ VISUAL DICTIONARY

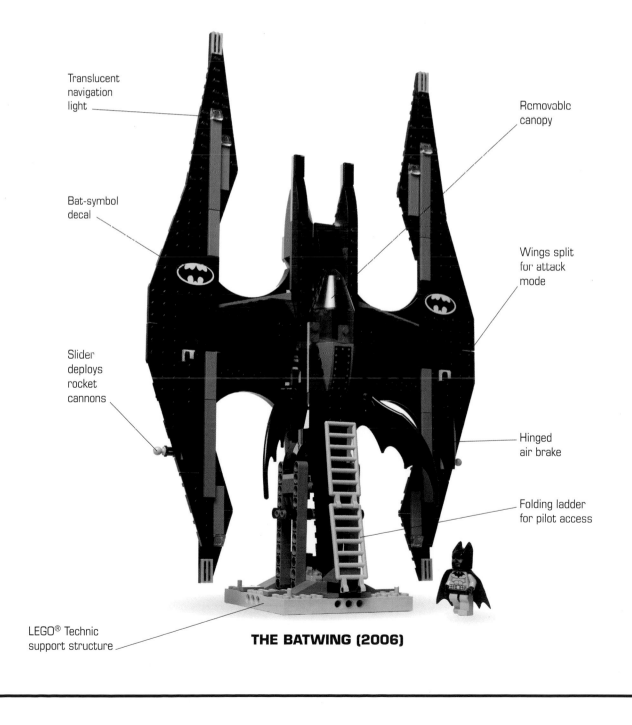

Translucent navigation light

Bat-symbol decal

Slider deploys rocket cannons

LEGO® Technic support structure

Removable canopy

Wings split for attack mode

Hinged air brake

Folding ladder for pilot access

THE BATWING (2006)

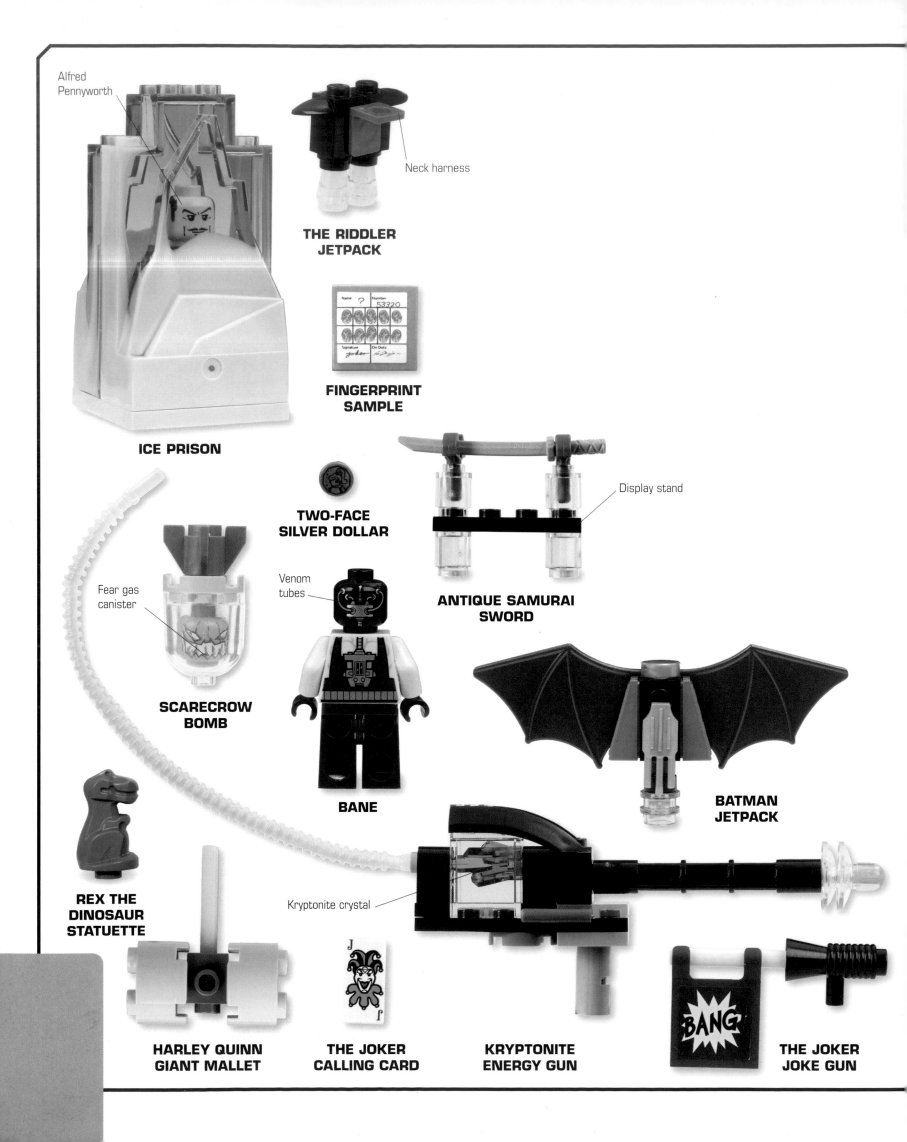

Alfred Pennyworth

ICE PRISON

Neck harness

THE RIDDLER JETPACK

FINGERPRINT SAMPLE

TWO-FACE SILVER DOLLAR

Display stand

ANTIQUE SAMURAI SWORD

Fear gas canister

SCARECROW BOMB

Venom tubes

BANE

BATMAN JETPACK

REX THE DINOSAUR STATUETTE

Kryptonite crystal

HARLEY QUINN GIANT MALLET

THE JOKER CALLING CARD

KRYPTONITE ENERGY GUN

THE JOKER JOKE GUN

DC UNIVERSE™
LEGO
SUPER HEROES

BATMAN™ VISUAL DICTIONARY

Written by Daniel Lipkowitz

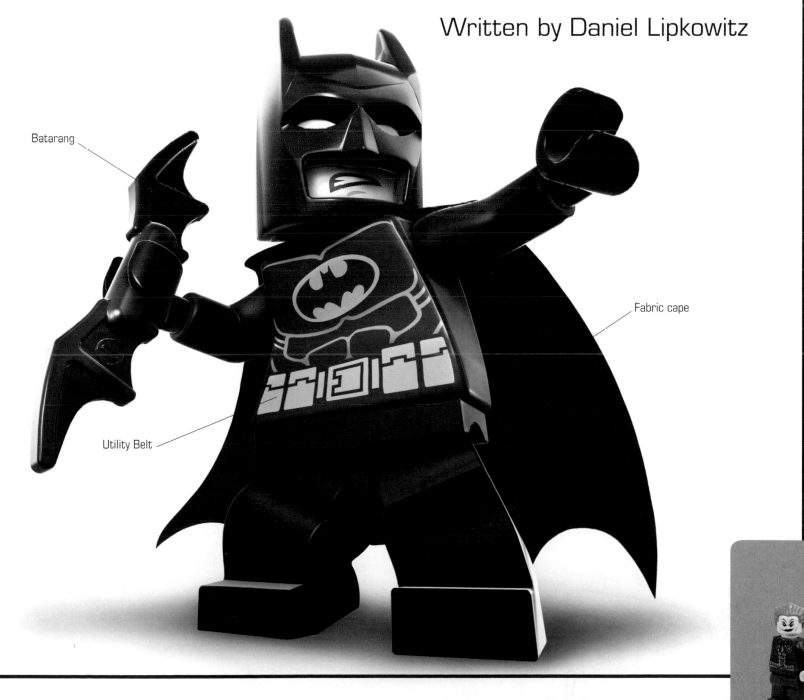

Batarang

Fabric cape

Utility Belt

CONTENTS

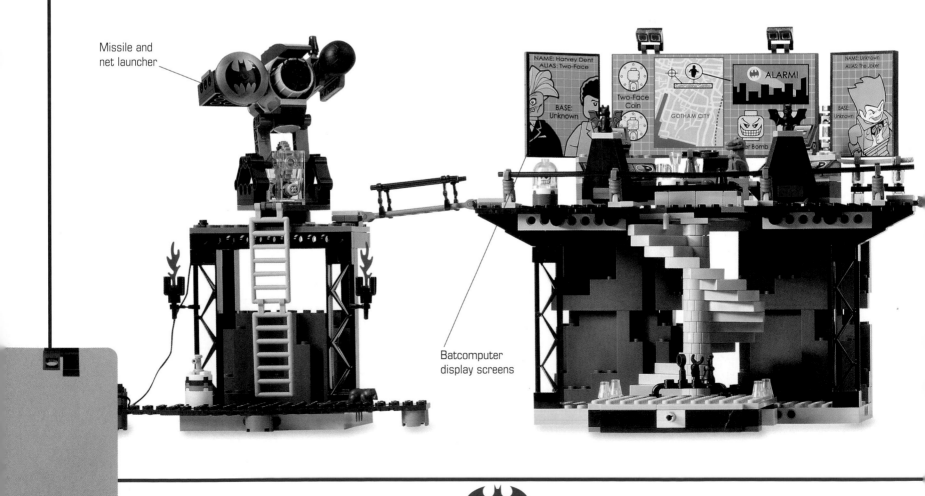

Missile and net launcher

Batcomputer display screens

NAME: Harvey Dent
ALIAS: Two-Face
BASE: Unknown

Two-Face Coin

GOTHAM CITY

ALARM!

NAME: Unknown
ALIAS: The Joker
BASE: Unknown

Batsuit changing pod

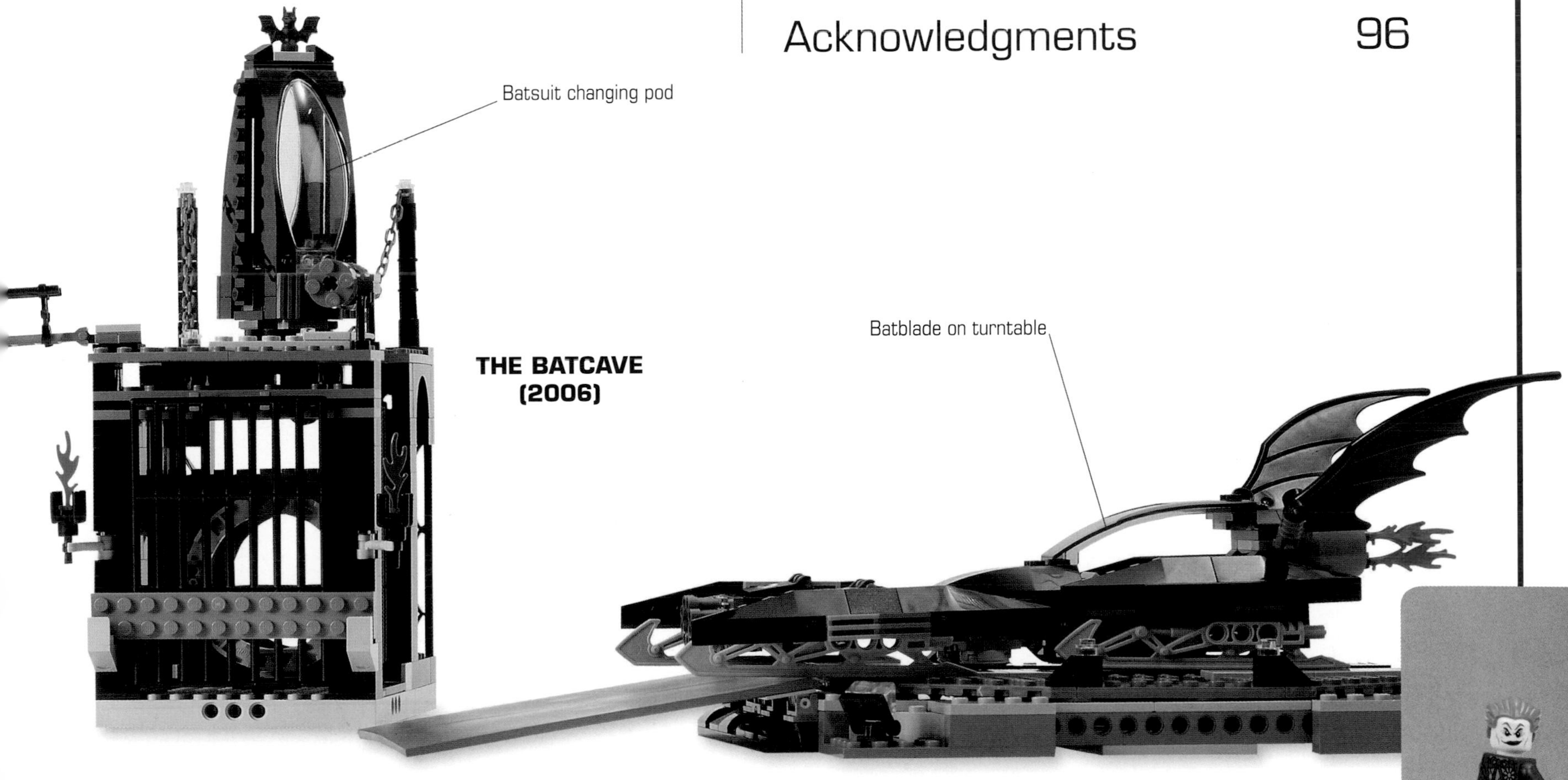

THE BATCAVE (2006)

Batblade on turntable

Gotham City Bank

BANK

Air vents

INTRODUCTION

Batman, also known as the Dark Knight and the Caped Crusader, has been capturing imaginations in comic books, animation, movies, and video games for generations. Creating the LEGO® Batman™ theme therefore required combining the character-rich world of DC Comics with sets packed with gadgets and hidden surprises, not to mention a wealth of rare black LEGO bricks. To the delight of kids and collectors alike, the new theme offered the chance to build some of Batman's most famous vehicles and locations, from the high-speed Batmobile to the top-secret Batcave.

Over the course of its initial three-year run, the line provided enough heroes, villains, and henchmen to populate your very own brick-built Gotham City—not to mention multiple versions of the Dark Knight himself.

The launch of the LEGO Super Heroes theme in 2012 not only marked the long-awaited return of LEGO Batman sets but also added other iconic characters from the DC Comics universe. Finally, you could create your own minifigure Justice League of America and team up to battle Lex Luthor, the Joker, and all their chaos-causing criminal cohorts!

Stolen bank safe

DATA FILE

Set Name: Batmobile and the Two-Face Chase

Year: 2012

Set Number: 6864

Pieces: 531

DATA FILES

Throughout the book, sets are identified with a data file (see example left), which provides the official name of the set, the year it was first released, the LEGO identification number of the set, the number of LEGO pieces, or elements, in each set (excluding minifigures).

Rotating chain gun

Monster truck wheels

TIMELINE

THE LEGO GROUP released its first LEGO® Batman™ sets in 2006, following the release of the movie *Batman Begins*. Models were inspired by both the original DC comic books and the new blockbuster movies. The original line ran from 2006-2008.

And just as the comic books have seen revisions over the years, so too have the LEGO sets. In early 2012 the line was relaunched, rebranded as LEGO DC Universe Super Heroes, featuring a new range of models and minifigures to delight fans of the movies, comic books, and LEGO sets alike...

▶ 2006

7779

THE BATMAN DRAGSTER: CATWOMAN PURSUIT

7780

THE BATBOAT: HUNT FOR KILLER CROC

7781

THE BATMOBILE: TWO-FACE'S ESCAPE

7782

THE BATWING: THE JOKER'S
AERIAL ASSAULT

7783

THE BATCAVE: THE PENGUIN AND
MR. FREEZE'S INVASION

7784

7785

THE BATMOBILE: ULTIMATE
COLLECTOR'S EDITION

ARKHAM ASYLUM

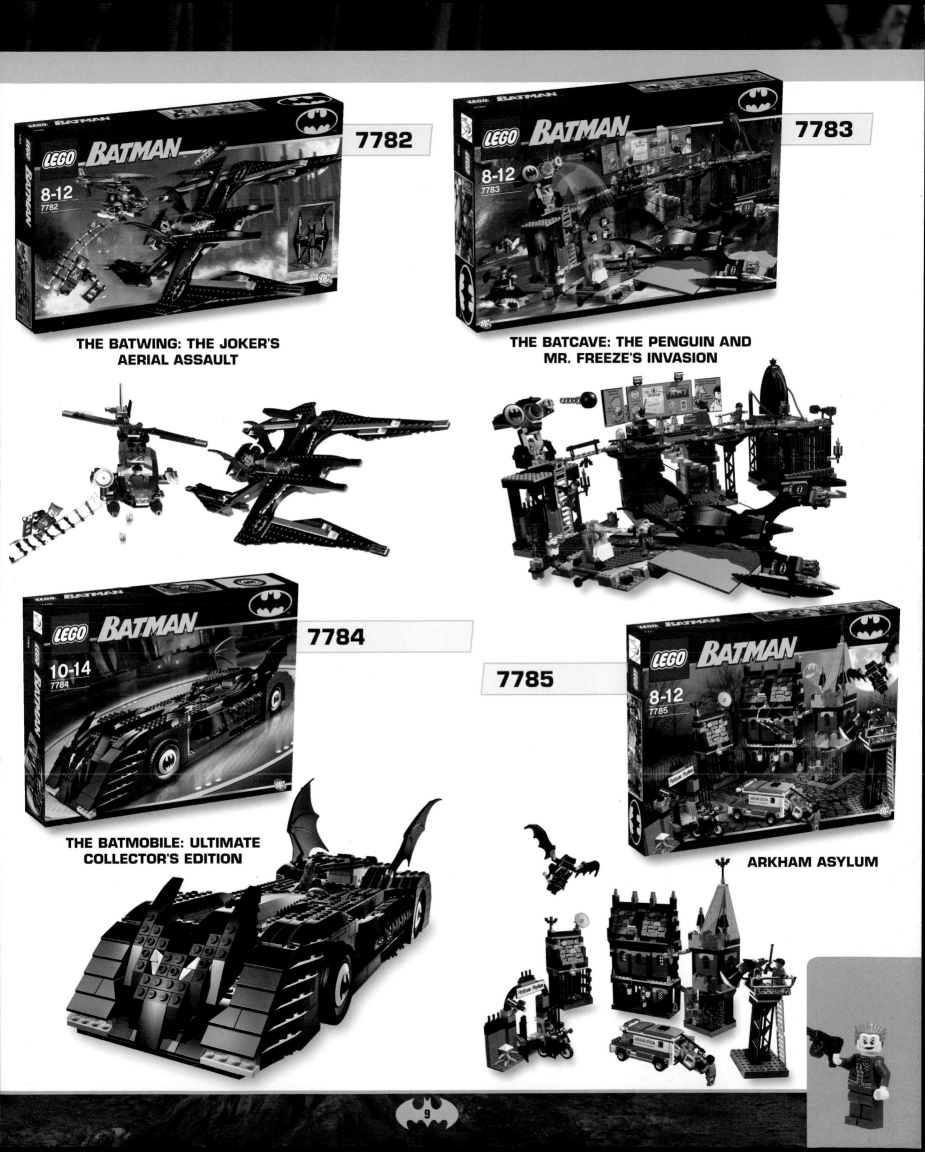

7786

7-12
7786

**THE BATCOPTER: THE CHASE
FOR SCARECROW**

7884

5-10
7884

**BATMAN'S BUGGY: THE
ESCAPE OF MR. FREEZE**

7787

8-12
7787

7885

7-12
7885

**THE BAT-TANK: THE RIDDLER
AND BANE'S HIDEOUT**

**ROBIN'S SCUBA JET:
ATTACK OF THE PENGUIN**

7886

THE BATCYCLE: HARLEY
QUINN'S HAMMER TRUCK

7888

THE TUMBLER: THE JOKER'S
ICE CREAM SURPRISE

4526

BATMAN

4527

THE JOKER

4528

GREEN
LANTERN

6857

**THE DYNAMIC DUO
FUNHOUSE ESCAPE**

6860

THE BATCAVE

6858

**CATWOMAN CATCYCLE
CITY CHASE**

6862

SUPERMAN VS. POWER ARMOR LEX

6863

BATWING BATTLE OVER GOTHAM CITY

6864

BATMOBILE AND THE TWO-FACE CHASE

30160

BAT JETSKI

30161

BATMOBILE

30164

LEX LUTHOR

LEGO® BATMAN™

LIGHT THE BAT-SIGNAL! From 2006 to 2008, the original series of LEGO® Batman™ sets provided the legendary defender of Gotham City with his very own fleet of sleek, high-tech vehicles and bat-themed crime-fighting gear. Not to be outdone, the Caped Crusader's classic foes were out in force as well—with an arsenal of rolling, flying, and diving rides customized in their personally unique styles. Good thing for the citizens of Gotham that Batman had a hidden Batcave headquarters and some of his greatest comic book allies by his side!

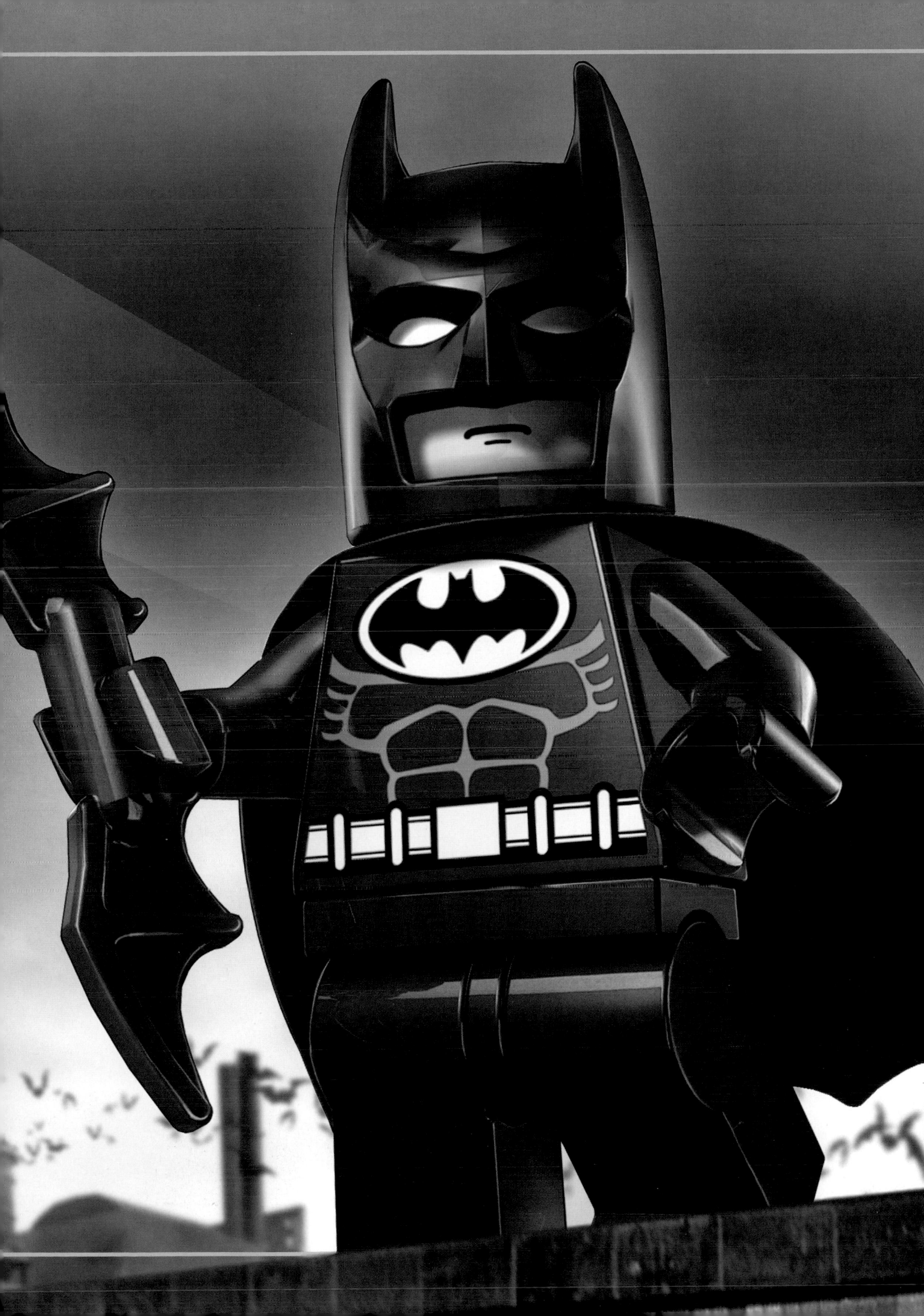

BATMAN

FROM HIS FIRST appearance as the mysterious masked "Batman" in 1939's *Detective Comics* #27, the Caped Crusader has solved mysteries, battled super-villains, and protected the citizens of Gotham City with a variety of costumes and equipment, all designed to strike fear into the hearts of superstitious criminals everywhere. The LEGO Batman theme followed suit with an assortment of Batman designs inspired by some of the hero's most famous looks in comics and film.

Removable cowl

Stylized bat-symbol on chest

High-tech modern Utility Belt

Cape mimics shape of bat wings

▶ Batman (2006)

Clad in classic black and gray, this version of Batman is based on his appearance in modern comics and cartoons. Like all LEGO Batman minifigures, beneath his helmet he features a printed face with a headband that creates the white eyes of the masked Dark Knight Detective.

ALFRED

Loyal and wise, Bruce Wayne's faithful butler Alfred takes care of not just Wayne Manor, but also the secret Batcave and its vehicles—not to mention Batman himself if he gets hurt in a fight!

He rarely smiles as Batman

◀ Bruce Wayne (2006)

In his secret identity, Batman is Bruce Wayne, a wealthy Gotham City businessman and head of Wayne Enterprises. Few suspect and even fewer know that the seemingly laid-back playboy has trained hard and devoted his life and fortune to fighting crime as the Caped Crusader. This Bruce Wayne minifigure is exclusive to set 7783 The Batcave: The Penguin and Mr. Freeze's Invasion.

Expensive business suit

BRICK FACTS

The 2006 Cartoon Network LEGO Batman: Bricks, Bats & Bad Guys mini-movie invited viewers to finish the story by choosing one of three possible endings!

Rubber-tipped launching missile

Intimidating headlight decals

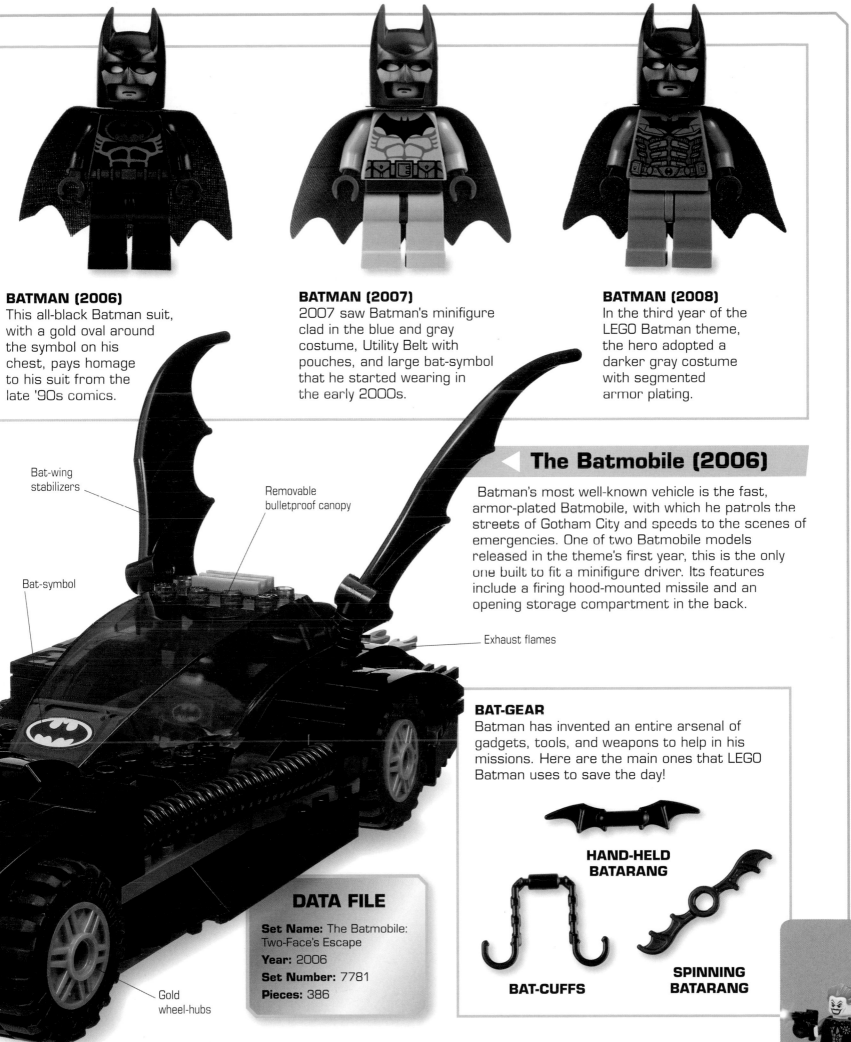

BATMAN (2006)
This all-black Batman suit, with a gold oval around the symbol on his chest, pays homage to his suit from the late '90s comics.

BATMAN (2007)
2007 saw Batman's minifigure clad in the blue and gray costume, Utility Belt with pouches, and large bat-symbol that he started wearing in the early 2000s.

BATMAN (2008)
In the third year of the LEGO Batman theme, the hero adopted a darker gray costume with segmented armor plating.

Bat-wing stabilizers

Removable bulletproof canopy

Bat-symbol

Exhaust flames

Gold wheel-hubs

◀ The Batmobile (2006)

Batman's most well-known vehicle is the fast, armor-plated Batmobile, with which he patrols the streets of Gotham City and speeds to the scenes of emergencies. One of two Batmobile models released in the theme's first year, this is the only one built to fit a minifigure driver. Its features include a firing hood-mounted missile and an opening storage compartment in the back.

BAT-GEAR
Batman has invented an entire arsenal of gadgets, tools, and weapons to help in his missions. Here are the main ones that LEGO Batman uses to save the day!

HAND-HELD BATARANG

SPINNING BATARANG

BAT-CUFFS

DATA FILE
Set Name: The Batmobile: Two-Face's Escape
Year: 2006
Set Number: 7781
Pieces: 386

THE BATMOBILE: ULTIMATE COLLECTORS' EDITION

COMICS, TELEVISION, and the movies have featured many different designs for the famous Batmobile, and so have the several LEGO sets in which it has appeared—but none are as big and detailed as The Batmobile: Ultimate Collectors' Edition from 2006, made from more than 1,000 pieces and stretching over 16 inches (42 cm) long!

Aerodynamically designed upper chassis

Bat-shield battering ram

DATA FILE

Set Name: The Batmobile: Ultimate Collectors' Edition

Year: 2006

Set Number: 7784

Pieces: 1045

Dimensions:
Length 16.75 in (42.5 cm)
Width 7.5 in (19 cm)
Height 8.6 in (22 cm)

Minifigures: None

Turbofan engine

Reinforced bulletproof chassis

Translucent yellow pieces for headlights

Air intake

Hood attachment point

▲ Batmobile

Ultimate Collector LEGO sets are designed for builders with plenty of experience, and the Batmobile is no exception. Packed with special functions, it makes an incredible display piece, though its black-brick-filled instructions can prove a challenge for even expert assemblers to follow.

18

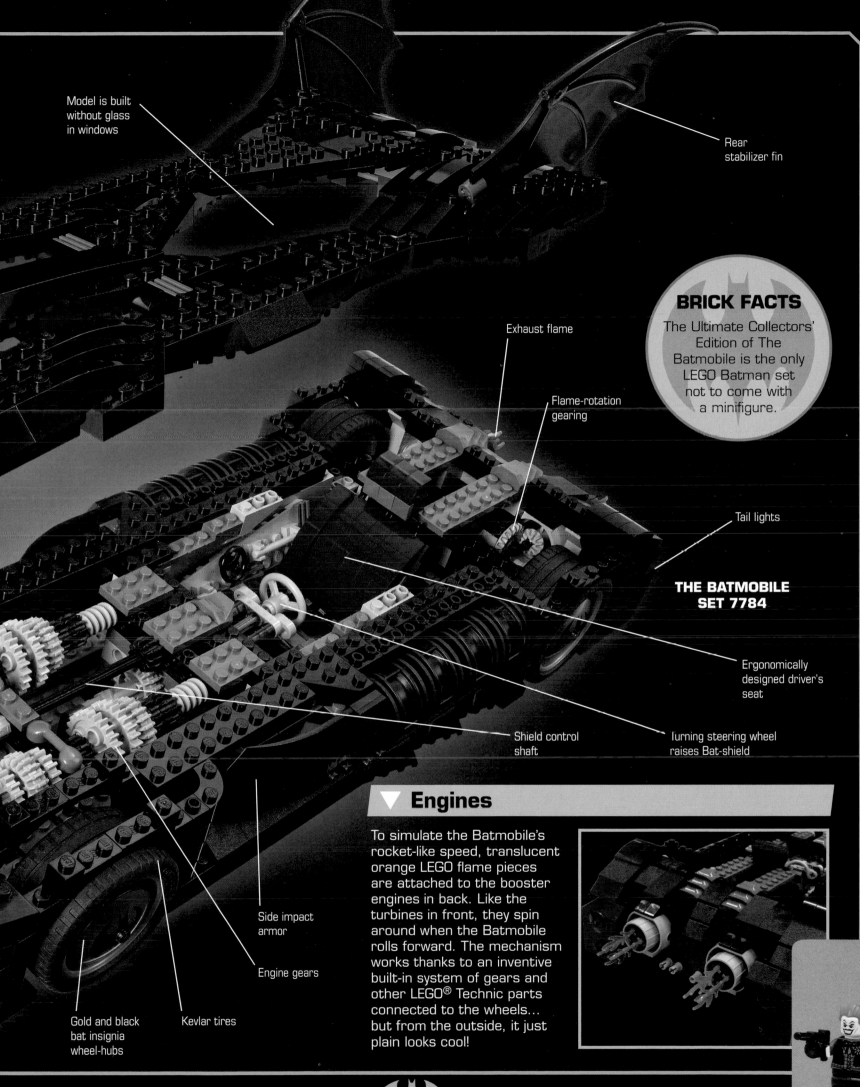

Model is built without glass in windows

Rear stabilizer fin

Exhaust flame

Flame-rotation gearing

Tail lights

**THE BATMOBILE
SET 7784**

Ergonomically designed driver's seat

Shield control shaft

Turning steering wheel raises Bat-shield

Side impact armor

Engine gears

Gold and black bat insignia wheel-hubs

Kevlar tires

▼ Engines

To simulate the Batmobile's rocket-like speed, translucent orange LEGO flame pieces are attached to the booster engines in back. Like the turbines in front, they spin around when the Batmobile rolls forward. The mechanism works thanks to an inventive built-in system of gears and other LEGO® Technic parts connected to the wheels... but from the outside, it just plain looks cool!

THE BATCAVE

HIDDEN IN the caverns deep beneath Wayne Manor is Batman's secret headquarters. Filled with some of the world's most high-tech crime-fighting equipment, this place is where the Dark Knight Detective stores all of his vehicles, studies up on super-villains, trains to keep himself in tip-top shape, and even displays trophies from some of his most challenging cases. Welcome to the Batcave!

DATA FILE

Set Name: The Batcave: The Penguin and Mr. Freeze's Invasion

Year: 2006

Set Number: 7783

Pieces: 1071

Refreshments for a hard-working Dark Knight

Floodlights

Missile launcher

High-res computer screen

Launcher controls

NAME: Harvey Dent ALIAS: Two-Face

Two-Face Coin

GOTHAM CITY

ALARM!

Joker Bomb

NAME: Unknown ALIAS: The Joker

BASE: Unknown

BASE: Unknown

Net launcher

Geared elevation mechanism

Connecting gangway

Deactivated Joker bomb

Spiral staircase

Tool rack

Flaming torch

Cave rat

Fuel tank

Batboat mooring point

BRICK FACTS

This is the only set in both the LEGO Batman and LEGO DC Universe Super Heroes themes to include a minifigure of Alfred the butler!

▼ The World of the Dark Knight

The original Batcave set is designed to tie the entire LEGO Batman world together. Not only does it have a self-contained action story about a break-in by Mr. Freeze and the Penguin, but its features are also built to interact with other models from the theme, like the dock for the Batboat and the rotating repair bay for the Batblade and Batmobile.

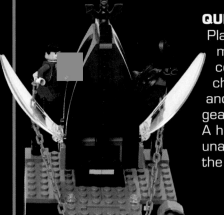

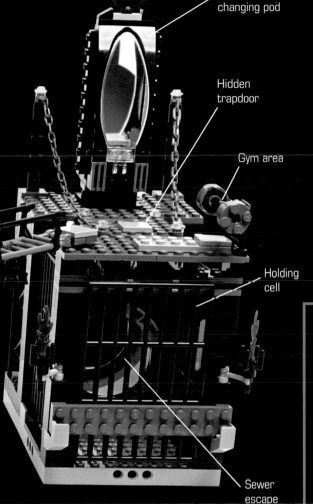

Batsuit changing pod

Hidden trapdoor

Gym area

Holding cell

Sewer escape pipe

Turntable for Batblade (see p.25)

Access ramp

Turntable control knob

▶ Security System

Few villains even know that the Batcave exists, but the ever-vigilant Batman has equipped it with a gear-aimed defense turret just in case. If the cave comes under attack, he can spot the trespassers with his Bat-Signal spotlight and then fire a spring-loaded rocket or launch a net to trap them.

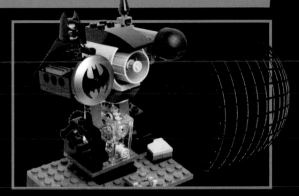

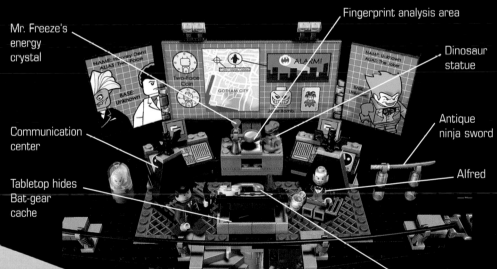

Mr. Freeze's energy crystal

Fingerprint analysis area

Dinosaur statue

Communication center

Antique ninja sword

Tabletop hides Bat-gear cache

Alfred

The Batphone

▲ Control Center

At the top of a flight of spiral stairs is the Batcave's state-of-the-art control center, where Batman analyzes clues with the help of his ultra-sophisticated Batcomputer. This vital section includes everything the Dark Knight needs to crack the clues and bring Gotham's criminals to justice, from collected evidence to comfy chairs and a tray of refreshments.

ARMORED BAT-VEHICLES

THE BAD GUYS don't always fight fair. Under threat from jack-in-the-box Joker bombs, Scarecrow fear gas grenades, and rocket-toting henchmen, Batman needs vehicles that will keep him safe in hazardous situations. Here are some of the Dark Knight's toughest vehicles, custom-built for smashing through gates, busting down barricades, and driving over anything that gets in their way!

▼ Bat-Tank

Facing a team-up of the Riddler's brain and Bane's brawn, Batman hops into the mighty Bat-Tank to take down the two villains. Combining a streamlined shape and sheer power, this original LEGO design features giant treads that are assembled one link at a time. When built, they really work!

Flick-fire missile

Hidden auto-firing missile

Working tank treads

Armor detail sticker

Reinforced sides protect tread components

Smooth, studless front end

Forward-pointing spikes

DATA FILE
Set Name: The Bat-Tank: The Riddler and Bane's Hideout
Year: 2007
Set Number: 7787
Pieces: 645

BAT-MISSILES
The Bat-Tank's triple missile launcher has two finger-flick rockets on the sides and a central rubber-tipped missile that automatically fires when you tilt it up.

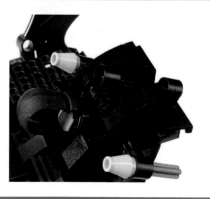

▼ Batblade

Another original vehicle created for the LEGO Batman line, the cold-weather Batblade is built to speed across frozen surfaces and blast through ice walls—a useful skill when your city is home to a super-villain called Mr. Freeze. It can only be found as part of the 2006 set 7783 The Batcave: The Penguin and Mr. Freeze's Invasion.

Rotating cannons built from LEGO binoculars

Pointed flamethrower nose

Blades for a smooth ride across ice

DATA FILE

Set Name: The Batcave: The Penguin and Mr. Freeze's Invasion

Year: 2006

Set Number: 7783

Pieces: 1071

BRICK FACTS

The Batblade's ice blades were originally created as tools for the hero Kopaka Nuva in the BIONICLE® theme.

▼ Tumbler

The only LEGO Batman set based exclusively on a movie vehicle, the Tumbler was first seen on screen in the 2005 film *Batman Begins*. The LEGO version captures all of the armored bulk and radar-reflecting angles of the military prototype from the movie, but with added side-mounted flick-firing rockets and a hidden missile launcher in back.

COCKPIT

Beneath its hinged roof, the Tumbler's roomy cockpit features seating for two, a steering wheel, an instrument panel, and an on-board computer display to help the Dark Knight win the advantage over the criminals of Gotham City.

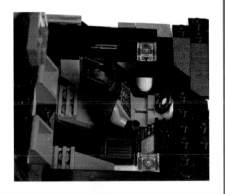

Adjustable rear flaps assist braking

Armored front for ramming enemy vehicles

Updated finger-flick rocket

Angled stealth armor

Autocannons

Oversized wheels roll over obstacles

DATA FILE

Set Name: The Tumbler: Joker's Ice Cream Surprise

Year: 2008

Set Number: 7888

Pieces: 449

SPEEDY WHEELS

OVERWHELMING STRENGTH and maximum armor aren't always the best way for the Dark Knight to get things done. Sometimes it's more important to get where you need to go at blazing fast speed if you want to protect the innocent and capture the crooks. That's why Batman keeps the Batcave well-stocked with some of the quickest rocket-propelled vehicles on the planet.

▼ Batman Dragster

Taking his cue from the high-powered vehicles used in drag races, Batman employs this unique three-wheeled auto for bursts of blinding speed across long stretches of flat terrain. It's well-armed for such a speedy racer: not only does the Dragster wield a pair of finger-fired flick missiles, but it also packs a spinning eight-barreled laser cannon in its pointy nose.

STEERING
Unlike most dragsters, which are designed to race in a straight line, the LEGO Batman Dragster makes use of a rotating LEGO plate to let its single front wheel swivel from side to side for tight high-speed turns.

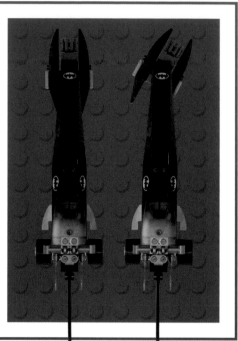

Flick-fire missile

Driver's cockpit

Long, tapering front end

Big rear wheels

Shield plates protect wheel

Air vents

REAR VIEW
When viewed from the back, it's clear where the Batman Dragster gets its speed from. It has a huge internal engine with a pair of flaming rocket boosters. Must be a hot seat for the Caped Crusader!

DATA FILE

Set Name: The Batman Dragster: Catwoman Pursuit
Year: 2006
Set Number: 7779
Pieces: 92

▶ Batman's Buggy

Batman uses this quick little Buggy when he chases the cold-blooded Mr. Freeze. What it lacks in size, it clearly makes up for in horsepower. Just check out its quadruple engine exhaust pipes and that plume of fire blasting out the back!

Central stabilizer fin

DATA FILE

Set Name: Batman's Buggy: The Escape of Mr. Freeze
Year: 2008
Set Number: 7884
Pieces: 76

Flame made from LEGO® BIONICLE fire sword

Smooth tires for speed

Swiveling harpoon launcher

Treaded tires for grip

Angled exhaust pipes

◀ Batcycle (2008)

When Harley Quinn goes on a mischievous crime spree in her hammer truck, Batman races to intercept her aboard his turbocharged Batcycle, decorated with a movie-style bat-symbol. This mighty motorcycle is solidly built with a swooping shape created by angled LEGO Technic beams, doubled-up tires for maximum stability, and two flick-fire missiles in case Harley somehow manages to outrun Gotham City justice.

Bat-wings made from LEGO dragon parts

Bat-symbol

DATA FILE

Set Name: The Batcycle: Harley Quinn's Hammer Truck
Year: 2008
Set Number: 7886
Pieces: 267

Rotating laser cannon

LEGO Technic beam

Double tires keep cycle balanced

BRICK FACTS
The Batcycle is ideally ... the motorcycle is made out of the Tumbler's front end!

AIR & SEA ATTACK

CROOKS AND SUPER-VILLAINS may try to hide in the most unusual places, but the Batman is always ready to track them down no matter where they are. From the speedy Batboat to the soaring Batwing jet, the Caped Crusader has built his own armada of floating and flying vehicles designed to rule the waters and skies of Gotham City—and anywhere else evil-doers go to cause havoc!

▼ Batwing (2006)

Batman has piloted a variety of Batplanes over the years, but few have looked as cool as the bat-shaped Batwing. Built to battle the Joker's helicopter, it is packed with secret weapons like slide-out double rocket cannons and a secret missile launcher that can deploy for battle or tuck away for streamlined supersonic flight.

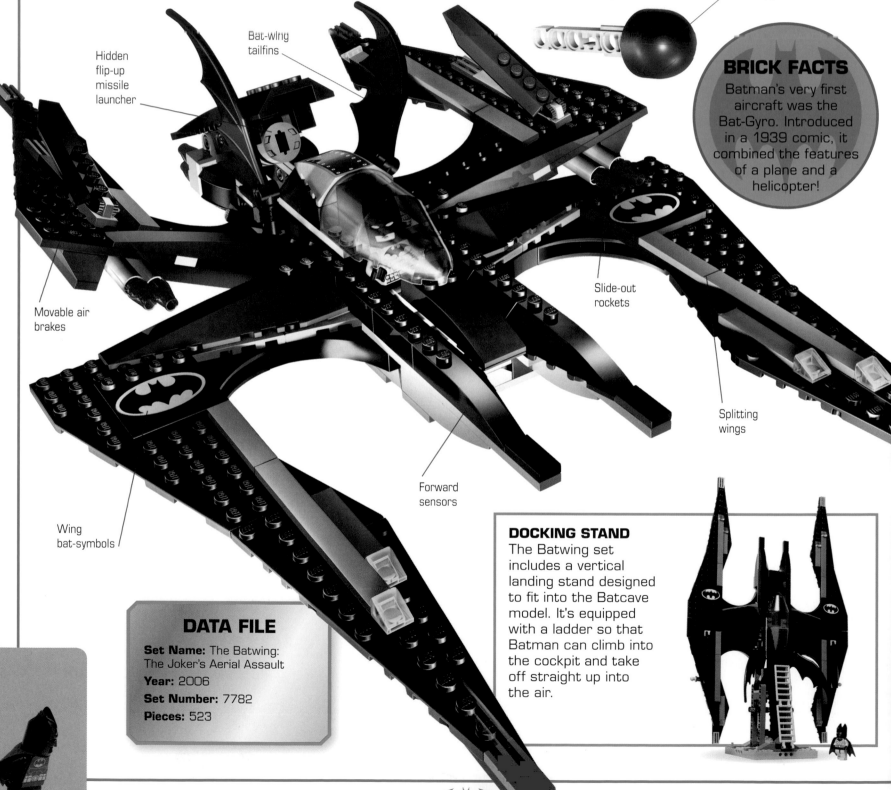

Rubber-tipped missile

Bat-wing tailfins

Hidden flip-up missile launcher

Movable air brakes

BRICK FACTS
Batman's very first aircraft was the Bat-Gyro. Introduced in a 1939 comic, it combined the features of a plane and a helicopter!

Slide-out rockets

Splitting wings

Forward sensors

Wing bat-symbols

DATA FILE

Set Name: The Batwing: The Joker's Aerial Assault

Year: 2006

Set Number: 7782

Pieces: 523

DOCKING STAND
The Batwing set includes a vertical landing stand designed to fit into the Batcave model. It's equipped with a ladder so that Batman can climb into the cockpit and take off straight up into the air.

DATA FILE

Set Name: The Batcopter: The Chase for Scarecrow

Year: 2007

Set Number: 7786

Pieces: 293

Triple-bladed rotor

Flick-launching rockets

Firing missile

▲ Batcopter

The high-tech Batcopter seems like more than a match for the Scarecrow's old-fashioned biplane (see p.39), but the Dark Knight is always thorough. This modern helicopter has all the latest weaponry, including a firing missile, two finger-flick rockets, and a pair of rotating cannons under the nose's sensor dome.

Rotating cannons

▶ Batglider

When the inmates of Arkham Asylum stage a breakout, Batman needs to make a quick aerial arrival using this small, stealthy glider. Its wings can be positioned using click-hinge joints, and its "tail" swings down to plug into the asylum's rooftop.

"Bat ears" on top

Poseable wings

Control handles

DATA FILE

Set Name: Arkham Asylum

Year: 2006

Set Number: 7785

Pieces: 860

▶ Batboat

With Killer Croc on a rampage in the swamps outside Gotham, Batman uses his hovercraft to sink his reptilian foe's plans. The Batboat's twin engines are linked so when you turn one, the other automatically rotates to point in the same direction.

Linked engines turn together

Spinning propeller fans

Spray-blocking canopy

Water cannons

DATA FILE

Set Name: The Batboat: Hunt for Killer Croc

Year: 2006

Set Number: 7780

Pieces: 188

Hovercraft skirt

Bright lights for spotting danger

SPEEDBOAT

If the Batboat gets damaged in action, Batman can escape aboard the miniature speedboat docked between its engines. Killer Croc's swamp jet ski (see p. 36) can also be attached there when it's time to tow his scaly hide back to prison!

ROBIN

ROBIN IS Batman's crime-fighting sidekick and most famous ally. With his brightly-colored uniform and cheerful smile, Robin is the fun-loving counterpoint to Batman's more serious personality. Several teenagers have worn Robin's cape over the years, but all of the LEGO versions have represented Tim Drake, the third Robin. Without the Boy Wonder at Batman's side, there wouldn't be a Dynamic Duo!

2008 HAIRSTYLE
The only difference between the 2006 and 2008 variants of the Robin minifigure is the new LEGO hair piece!

▼ Robin's Scuba Jet

Robin gets to be the hero all on his own in this Batman-free set, which pits his personal high-speed scuba jet in an underwater duel against the Penguin's newest penguin-sub. Just like Batman's vehicles and equipment share the Dark Knight's colors and bat theme, Robin's vehicles echo the look of his red, green, and yellow costume.

DATA FILE
Set Name: Robin's Scuba Jet: Attack of the Penguin
Year: 2008
Set Number: 7885
Pieces: 207

Robin's symbol

Aerodynamic fin

Spinning propeller

Removable canopy

Hydro-blaster

Aqua-turbine engine

Robin (2006)

Tim Drake first showed off his amazing detective skills when he figured out Batman's secret identity—proving that he was worthy of being the new Robin. His LEGO minifigure represents Tim's original and most famous costume, the first Robin outfit to feature long pants instead of shorts. Robin was released twice in the LEGO Batman theme: in 2006 and 2008.

Rotating cannon

Joystick

Wavy hair

Armor-lined vest

Streamlined shape for extra speed

Adjustable side-wings

Hull-piercing spikes

Robin's Jetski

It may be the smallest vehicle in the giant Batcave set (2006), but Robin's colorful jetski is definitely the most eye-catching model in the set. The Boy Wonder is once again up against the Penguin and a penguin-shaped submarine. Apparently birds of a feather really do flock—or is that fight—together!

DATA FILE

Set Name:
The Batcave:
The Penguin and
Mr. Freeze's Invasion
Year: 2006
Set Number: 7783
Pieces: 1071

Escrima fighting sticks

Nightwing

Nightwing symbol

Rocket exhaust

DATA FILE

Set Name:
Arkham Asylum
Year: 2006
Set Number: 7785
Pieces: 860

Dark armor plating

NIGHTWING

Dick Grayson was the original Robin in the DC comics, a trained circus acrobat who joined Batman's battle against crime. When he grew older, he struck out on his own as the hero Nightwing, but he still comes to Batman's aid when needed. Nightwing's minifigure wears one of his more modern costumes, a far cry from his original high-collared, disco-inspired suit.

"Bang!" gag gun

Acid-squirting flower

THE JOKER

TRANSFORMED BY a fall into a chemical bath, a minor crook was changed forever. His skin became stark white, his face was scarred with a perpetual grin, and his mind gained a uniquely warped outlook on life. Calling himself the Joker, the self-titled Clown Prince of Crime embarked on a life of lawbreaking in which all of his schemes and gadgets have a joke theme—though the Joker is usually the only one laughing!

▲ The Joker (2006)

The Joker's minifigure wears a purple suit with an orange vest and green tie. His head is white plastic with a spiky hair piece molded in green. He was first made available at San Diego Comic-Con 2005 in a special talking box (that also included a Batman minifigure), which announced the upcoming LEGO Batman line and was limited to just 250 copies.

DATA FILE

Set Name: The Tumbler: Joker's Ice Cream Surprise
Year: 2008
Set Number: 7888
Pieces: 449

A TRICKY TREAT
What's the secret surprise concealed inside the Joker's truck? Push down on the ice cream cone on top and a hidden missile blasts out through the hinged rear doors!

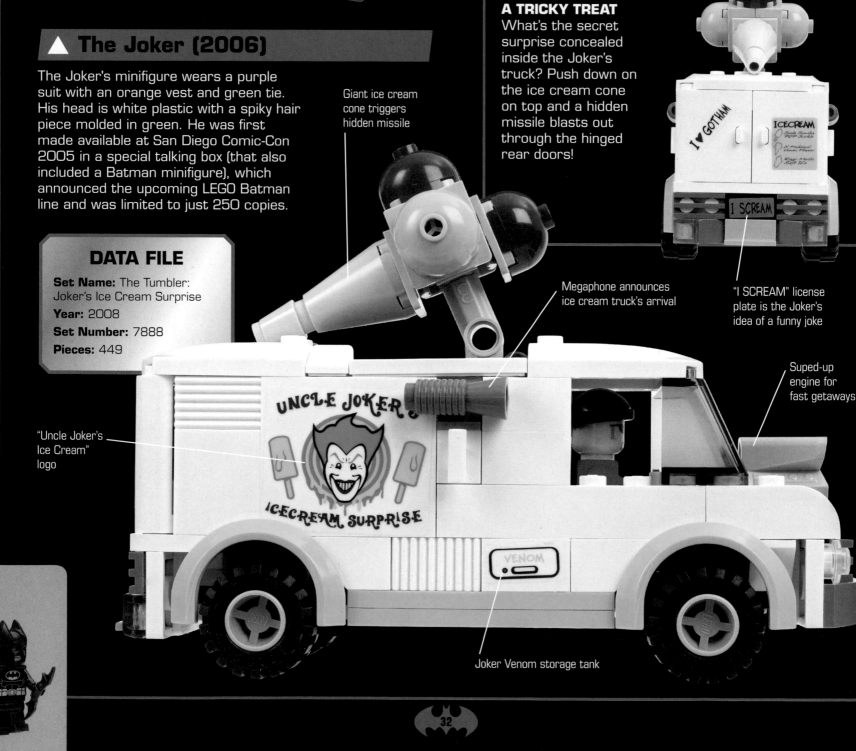

Giant ice cream cone triggers hidden missile

Megaphone announces ice cream truck's arrival

"I SCREAM" license plate is the Joker's idea of a funny joke

"Uncle Joker's Ice Cream" logo

Suped-up engine for fast getaways

Joker Venom storage tank

Knit cap

Spinning rotor

DATA FILE

Set Name: The Batwing: The Joker's Aerial Assault
Year: 2006
Set Number: 7782
Pieces: 523

Joker Venom popsicle

Spotlight drops ladder

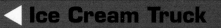
▲ Henchman (2006)

Not every criminal in Gotham City is a super-villain. For every Scarecrow or Penguin, there are dozens of low-level crooks ready to sell their services to the bigger bad guys to make a quick buck. This minifigure is one of those: a purple-shirted henchman who helps the Joker with his zany plans and crazy schemes.

▲ The Joker Copter (2006)

The Joker dangles from his helicopter's ladder high above Gotham City's skyline. Decorated with the crazed clown's face and color scheme, the Joker Copter has a built-in lever for dropping laughing gas bombs. When the Batwing's missile hits the spotlight mounted next to the cockpit, it releases the ladder, sending the Joker tumbling into the hands of justice.

Ladder built from LEGO ropes connected by robot arms

Joker's gun made from megaphone element

BRICK FACTS

The LEGO designers tried lots of different hairstyles for the Joker before finally settling on a vampire hair piece from the LEGO® Studios line!

◀ Ice Cream Truck

The Joker is on the loose in Gotham City once again! This time, he's hatched a fiendish plan to make the citizens smile (whether they want to or not) by selling ice cream treats laced with laugh-inducing Joker Venom. His truck is covered with custom decals and packs an unexpected defense against any pursuing Dark Knights.

LAUGHING GAS BOMB

JOKER CARD

THE PENGUIN

OSWALD COBBLEPOT is one of Batman's oldest—and oddest—foes. Always impeccably dressed, he presents himself as an upstanding Gotham City citizen while secretly plotting robberies and heists with his signature combination of trick umbrellas and bird-themed gimmicks. Fortunately, the Dark Knight is always ready to stop the "Gentleman of Crime" and throw this bird behind bars!

Trick umbrella (hides a parachute, blaster, or anything else)

Elegant tuxedo pattern

▲ The Penguin

The Penguin's minifigure wears a monocle over one eye and is dressed in his customary tuxedo with purple bow tie, white gloves, and a removable top hat. The Penguin has always been conscious of his small stature, and his minifigure is the same—thanks to short, unposeable legs. He carries a trick umbrella, built out of a bar element and a radar dish.

◀ Foul Fowls

Other villains might employ human henchmen, but the Penguin relies on a squad of trained penguin minions to help him carry out his dirty deeds. Included in both of the Penguin's sets, these pistol-packing (and sometimes harpoon-holding) avians of avarice are each built out of eight black, white, red, and yellow LEGO pieces.

Clip holds weapon handle

INSIDE ACCESS
The sub's sides open to let the Penguin stand inside when it's under water. Interior details include the periscope's sight, a printed gauge, and a control handle.

Spinning propeller

Ungentlemanly armament

Movable periscope

Torpedo tubes

U98

DATA FILE

Set Name: The Batcave: The Penguin and Mr. Freeze's Invasion
Year: 2006
Set Number: 7783
Pieces: 1071

▶ The Penguin Sub—U98

An underground river allows Batman's water vehicles to enter and exit the Batcave—and the Penguin thinks it's the perfect way to launch his own submersible sneak attack! The Penguin's first submarine is built to resemble a real diving penguin, with a beak, flippers, and even articulated feet in back for steering. Its periscope can be raised and lowered.

The Penguin Sub—U99

The Penguin returns at the controls of a second, larger sub, which he uses for a daring underwater diamond heist. With its more realistic submarine design, this updated version relies on colored bricks and decals to provide its penguin-like appearance. The top deck pops off to reveal a pilot cabin fitted with a sonar readout.

Periscope raises and rotates

Removable top deck

Flick-fire rockets

DATA FILE

Set Name: Robin's Scuba Jet: Attack of the Penguin
Year: 2008
Set Number: 7885
Pieces: 207

Stolen diamond

Porthole sticker

Penguin face decal

Tally of Bat-vehicles sunk (four so far!)

Rubber-tipped torpedo

REAR VIEW

The Penguin's new sub is ready to send Robin's scuba jet to Davy Jones's locker with a rear-mounted torpedo that elevates and fires at the pull of a lever. When all his mischief has been completed, the Penguin can make use of the sub's giant turbine engines to make a quick getaway... unless he finds himself pursued by the Dynamic Duo, of course!

Rotating turbine

CATWOMAN & KILLER CROC

SELINA KYLE, the whip-wielding Catwoman, is a complicated character. With a penchant for jewel robberies and cat-themed crimes since her 1940 comic book debut, the larcenous and sneaky cat burglar has been both an enemy to the Dark Knight and a close friend and ally. One thing's for sure: where this capable kitty is concerned, you never know what to expect!

Flame element for extra speed

Cats-eyes sticker

DATA FILE

Set Name: The Batman Dragster: Catwoman Pursuit
Year: 2006
Set Number: 7779
Pieces: 245

Dark purple motorcycle fairing

▲ Catwoman's Motorbike (2006)

Just like her cat-themed minifigure costumes, Catwoman's accessories also have a recurring feline motif. The rocket-powered motorbike that she uses to try to elude Batman's speedy Dragster in a chase through the streets of Gotham has cat-ear-shaped side mirrors and distinctive yellow cats-eyes that can be applied as stickers. She'll definitely give Batman a run for his money in a high-speed city chase!

▼ Catwoman (2006)

Mask hides Catwoman's true identity

Catwoman's first minifigure features her dressed in the costume found in her most recent comic book incarnation: a stealthy black catsuit that makes nighttime misadventures and break-ins a breeze. Her trusty whip helps her swing around Gotham City and tangle up anyone—hero or villain—who gets in her way.

BRICK FACTS

Catwoman's Motorbike is built with a rare purple fairing—purple classically being of the cat burglar's favorite colors!

Spinning propeller

Swamp-camouflage color scheme

Black whip, adapted from a LEGO plant vine element

▶ Killer Croc

Predatory teeth

Red reptilian eyes

Scaly green skin

Printed crocodile cowling

KILLER CROC

DATA FILE

Set Name: The Batboat: Hunt for Killer Croc
Year: 2006
Set Number: 7780
Pieces: 188

Finger-flick missiles

Killer Croc (real name Waylon Jones) has gone through a lot of changes in his lawbreaking life. When he first showed up, he just had a bad skin condition, but these days he's got the appearance, strength, and ferocity of a real reptile—and his minifigure has a swamp jet ski to match.

HARLEY QUINN

ONCE UPON a time, Dr. Harleen Quinzel was a psychiatrist working at Arkham Asylum—until the Joker became her patient. Falling in love with her "Mister J," she helped him escape, and joined him on his fiendish felonies as the brightly-costumed Harley Quinn. For all her lawbreaking behavior, Harley isn't altogether bad—she just thinks the rest of the world doesn't get the joke!

SPIN 'N' SLAM
Harley's hammer is controlled by twisting a knob at the back of the truck. She has even included a bumper sticker with a special message for her favorite clown.

"Whack-A-Bat" hammer for squashing pesky Caped Crusading minifigures

Exposed custom engine

▶ Harley's Hammer Truck

Harley's monster truck is built to cause as much mayhem as possible. Its giant wheels drive over obstacles (like Gotham City police cars), and a pair of flick-fire missiles in back help take care of anything bigger in its way. Most devastating of all is the giant hammer that swings from side to side to smash any Bat-vehicles that get too close.

Giant monster truck tires

▽ Harley Quinn (2006)

Animation-style costume with printed puffy collar

REVOLVER

MISSILES

MALLET

CRATE OF JEWELS

With a mischievous grin and an oversized mallet, the first Harley Quinn minifigure wears her famous two-toned harlequin costume from the *Batman: The Animated Series* TV show where she first appeared. A fan-favorite character, her arrival two years into the LEGO Batman theme was very well received.

DATA FILE

Set Name: The Batcycle: Harley Quinn's Hammer Truck

Year: 2008

Set Number: 7886

Pieces: 188

Helmet keeps the heat out and the cold in

Goggles protect sensitive eyes

MR. FREEZE

DR. VICTOR FRIES was a simple scientist until an accident permanently lowered his body temperature and forced him to wear a special suit and helmet to survive. Now he uses special ice-generating technology to commit cold-based crimes as the frozen-hearted Mr. Freeze. Batman risks a lot more than catching a cold when he tangles with this sub-zero super-villain!

Freeze blaster encases victims in ice

Thermo-regulatory suit control chest piece last seen on a LEGO minifigure in 1991

BRICK FACTS

Mr. Freeze's helmet originated in the LEGO® Space Insectoids theme in 1998, but this was the first time it was produced in this color.

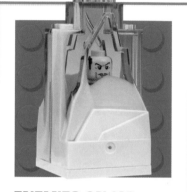

▲ Mr. Freeze

Mr. Freeze first appeared as a minifigure in 7783 The Batcave: The Penguin and Mr. Freeze's Invasion. He carries a large buildable freeze blaster with a hose that plugs into his ice-generating backpack. Only his head has special decoration; his torso is plain blue under his removable chest piece.

Diamond power source

Power conduit cable

ENEMIES ON ICE

The 2006 Batcave also features two transparent ice block pieces and a white base plate that combine to make a frozen prison for an unfortunate minifigure.

DATA FILE

Set Name:
Batman's Buggy: The Escape of Mr. Freeze

Year: 2008

Set Number: 7884

Pieces: 76

Knitted hat

COLD-WEATHER CROOK

It must be chilly having Mr. Freeze as a boss! His color-coded henchman has the same torso, but gray legs and a face shared with other low-life LEGO goons.

The henchman sure likes his weaponry!

Smooth wheels speed over ice

Two-tone ice blast effect

▲ Sub-zero Speedster

Also known as Mr. Freeze's Kart in LEGO *Batman: The Videogame*, this small vehicle lets Mr. Freeze try to escape from Batman with the stolen diamonds he needs to power his ice ray. The Mr. Freeze minifigure included is identical to the first version, but his freeze blaster has a different construction.

THE SCARECROW

WHAT IS IT WITH all these evil doctors? Psychology professor Dr. Jonathan Crane was fascinated with the effect of fear. That's why he decided to dress up like a spooky scarecrow and use fear gas and chemicals to give his foes horrifying hallucinations. There's only one thing that gives the Scarecrow nightmares, and that's being caught by Batman and thrown back in Arkham Asylum!

BOMBS AWAY!

Swing down the lever and Scarecrow's plane drops a pair of buildable fear gas bombs. Inside each one is a minifigure head decorated like a creepy jack-o-lantern with a fiery bat-shaped mouth!

Fear gas canister

Bomb release lever

DATA FILE

Set Name: The Batcopter: The Chase for Scarecrow
Year: 2007
Set Number: 7786
Pieces: 293

The Scarecrow's Biplane

The Scarecrow has stolen and customized a cropduster plane to spray fear gas all across Gotham City. The villain's method of flight may be old-fashioned, but it'll take some of Batman's most high-tech equipment to clean up the city after this battle! Scarecrow's biplane is colored brown to match its pilot and features storage clips for his scythe and guns, a spinning propeller, and a bomb-dropping mechanism.

Scarecrow mask tailfin sticker

Spinning propeller

Pointed black hat

Glow-in-the-dark head

Rear-facing pistol

Machine gun

Clothes made of sewn-together rags

Sinister stitched scarecrow mask

The Scarecrow

SCYTHE

FEAR GAS BOMB

The Scarecrow minifigure's torso has printed stitching, a rope belt, and the tattered bottom of the villain's mask. His hat was originally made for LEGO® Castle witches and wizards. His most unusual feature is his translucent head, which glows in the dark! The Scarecrow also appeared in the 2006 Arkham Asylum set with the same design but a differently-built scythe.

BANE

BATMAN MAY NOT have super-strength, but some of his villains come a lot tougher than the average crook. The Dark Knight has to keep both his mind and his muscles keenly trained at all times to go up against a powerful bruiser like the muscle-bound Bane. This is one character that you definitely wouldn't want to bump into in a blind alley!

▶ Bane (2007)

Don't be fooled by Bane's brutish appearance: he's actually one of Batman's smartest foes. And when he's powered-up by strength-enhancing Venom, he's one of the strongest, too! Bane's original minifigure is covered with printed detail, from his bulging muscles and scars beneath his blue costume, to his zipped black mask with red eyes.

BANE'S BACK
Bane's printing continues on his back, depicting the Venom dispenser that pumps the chemicals into the back of his mask.

Silver Utility Belt

Rotating and tilting spotlight

Chain "locks" gate shut

"No Bats" warning sign

Remote-control machine gun

▲ The Riddler & Bane's Hideout

Bane has teamed up with the Riddler to brew up some trouble for Gotham City behind the gates of their well-defended hideout. With their collection of explosives, chemicals, and counterfeit money, they've got all the bad-guy bases covered, so it's a good thing Batman has brought his Bat-Tank for the big showdown. It might be the only vehicle that can actually get past Bane!

DETONATOR

CHEMICAL CANISTER

COUNTERFEIT MONEY

DYNAMITE

▼ Bane's Bike

Bane patrols the Riddler's counterfeiting operation on a heavily-armed, three-wheeled dirt bike with a big side-cannon and flick-missiles. Better hope the Bat-Tank's armor is as tough as it looks!

Weapon power supply

Dirt-busting tires

Rotating cannon

DATA FILE

Set Name: The Bat-Tank: The Riddler and Bane's Hideout
Year: 2007
Set Number: 7787
Pieces: 645

TWO-FACE

THE TRAGIC TALE of one of Batman's most doubly-dangerous adversaries begins with district attorney Harvey Dent. When half of his face was scarred by acid, his personality split, transforming him into the gangster Two-Face. Now he makes all of his decisions by flipping a coin to decide if he'll be bad or good—and bad seems to win most of the time!

Unique hair piece exclusive to Two-Face's minifigures

"Good" Harvey Dent half

"Bad" Two-Face half

Expensively tailored suit

▶ Two-Face (2006)

How do you make a minifigure of a character who looks like he's been split down the middle? Give him one black leg, one black arm, one gray hand, and a brand-new hair piece. He has an asymmetric face print and a suit with two-toned printing on the front and back. The first Two-Face minifigure's fashion sense was inspired by his classy black-and-white outfit from *Batman: The Animated Series*.

HIRED HELP
Two-Face's henchman wears a two-toned shirt to match his employer. Two-Face usually does everything in pairs, but maybe this solo goon is double trouble.

▼ Two-Face's Armored Car

This getaway vehicle may look like an ordinary Gotham City Bank truck, but one of the coins in its logo is scratched-up, and its color scheme is split down the middle. It also has twin cannons hidden in its sides. When the Batmobile's missile hits the back, anyone standing on top goes flying!

Armor-plated sticker on windshield

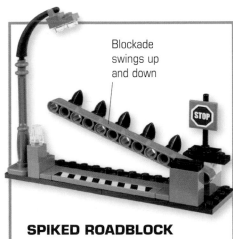

Blockade swings up and down

Flip-down panel reveals cannon

SPIKED ROADBLOCK
If this roadblock can't stop Two-Face, maybe Batman's tire-popping spiked chain can!

DATA FILE
Set Name: The Batmobile: Two-Face's Escape
Year: 2006
Set Number: 7781
Pieces: 386

Two headlights on each side

ARKHAM ASYLUM

WHAT DO you do when you've captured a super-villain? Most of Gotham City's biggest crooks are a little too unhinged for ordinary jail. Instead, they're locked up at Arkham Asylum, a gothic and gloomy-looking high-security hospital where it's hoped that the staff of doctors and psychiatrists will help them become sane and productive citizens. Unfortunately for Batman, they usually just escape to cause even more chaos!

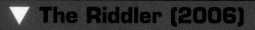
Edward Nigma loves puzzles and word games. As the Riddler, he always leaves complicated clues to his crimes for Batman to figure out in order to stop him. The Riddler's first minifigure wears his traditional green question-mark costume.

▼ Inside the Asylum

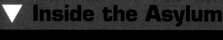

No one ever said Arkham was a fun place to visit, and it's definitely not a nice place to stay. This equipment is supposed to help treat the asylum's infamous inmates, but some of it seems just a little over the top. No wonder the villains who get sent here always try to leave so soon.

BRICK FACTS
There are cell doors within Arkham labeled "The Penguin" and "Mr. Freeze"—even though those minifigures don't appear in this set!

Satellite dish

Guard equipment storage

Security camera watches over front gate

Riddler's cell floor displays his obsession with puzzles

▼ Poison Ivy (2006)

Pamela Isley has always liked plants more than people. She may be a brilliant botanist, but she uses her knowledge of floral toxins and vegetable hybrids to commit ecological crimes, making Poison Ivy one of Batman's most dangerous foes. Even her 2006 minifigure costume is made out of plants!

Nightwing riding Nightcycle

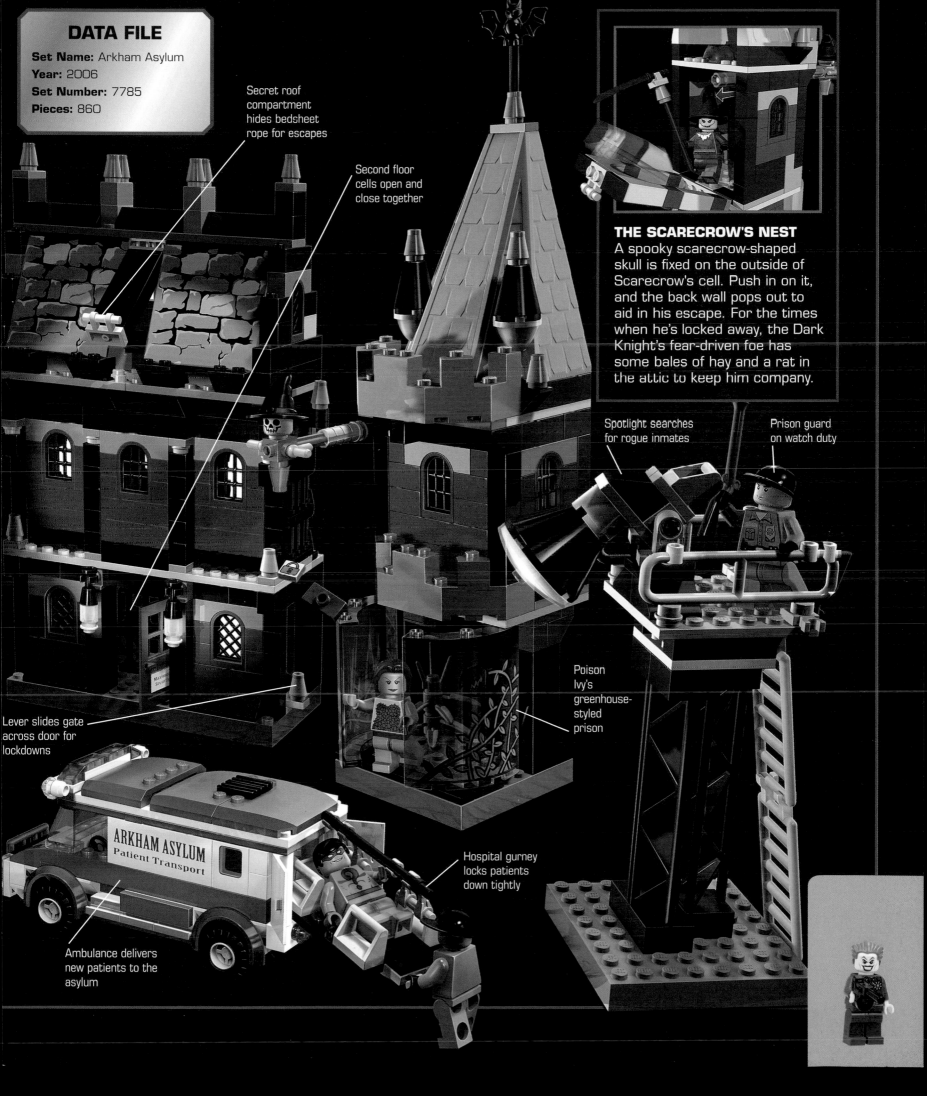

DATA FILE

Set Name: Arkham Asylum
Year: 2006
Set Number: 7785
Pieces: 860

Secret roof compartment hides bedsheet rope for escapes

Second floor cells open and close together

THE SCARECROW'S NEST

A spooky scarecrow-shaped skull is fixed on the outside of Scarecrow's cell. Push in on it, and the back wall pops out to aid in his escape. For the times when he's locked away, the Dark Knight's fear-driven foe has some bales of hay and a rat in the attic to keep him company.

Spotlight searches for rogue inmates

Prison guard on watch duty

Poison Ivy's greenhouse-styled prison

Lever slides gate across door for lockdowns

ARKHAM ASYLUM
Patient Transport

Hospital gurney locks patients down tightly

Ambulance delivers new patients to the asylum

LEGO® DC SUPER HEROES

SUPER HEROES UNITE! When Batman returned to the world of LEGO® building in 2012, he didn't come alone. Along with new versions of the Batcave and the Batmobile were a host of re-imagined allies and enemies, plus the very first LEGO sets starring superpowered heroes from other corners of the DC Universe. Superman, Wonder Woman, and a convention-exclusive Green Lantern were just the start, joining forces with the Dark Knight to form the core of a mighty minifigure Justice League that would make even the villainous Lex Luthor shake in his Kryptonite-powered mecha-boots!

BATMAN (2012)

THE NEW LEGO® DC Universe Super Heroes theme has expanded to include the entire universe of DC Comics, but Batman is definitely still the star of the show. Out of all the LEGO sets in the theme's debut year, there's only one that doesn't star the Dark Knight himself. After all, nobody else has the variety of equipment, vehicles, and building potential of Batman!

Translucent rocket trail doubles as support stand

Jet booster core

▶ Batman Jetpack

When the mission calls for speed over size, Batman straps on his bat-winged jetpack and takes to the skies. With a new plastic wing element that replaces his familiar cape and a rocket booster in back, Batman is all set to chase down Catwoman and put a stop to her latest jewel theft.

Plastic glider wing-pack

Batarang

GIVEAWAY
The first Batman minifigure in the new line is this limited-edition movie-based version, which was originally given away to lucky fans at the LEGO booth at the San Diego Comic-Con in 2011.

▼ Batsuits (2012)

The main theme includes two new Batman costume variants: a gray and blue Batsuit based on his classic comic-book look from the 1960s–1990s, and an all-black version similar to the one he started wearing in 1995. Both have removable masks and share the same double-sided head.

◀ Bruce Wayne (2012)

Just like in 2006, Batman's alter ego Bruce Wayne is only available in minifigure form as part of a big Batcave set. With a lighter blue suit and a much sterner expression than the original version, Bruce looks ready to don his crime-fighting gear at a moment's notice.

ROBIN RETURNS
Tim Drake adopted this red-and-black costume in honor of Superboy. His double-sided 2012 head features a smirk and a look of alarm.

DATA FILE

Set Name: Batmobile and the Two-Face Chase

Year: 2012

Set Number: 6864

Pieces: 531

Angled bat-wing tailfins

Rocket flames

Exhaust pipes

Opening canopy

Silver grille elements

EXCLUSIVE

Only available with the trade edition of *LEGO Batman: The Visual Dictionary*, this special-edition Batman minifigure wears the Electro Suit that helps him solve puzzles in the LEGO *Batman 2* video game.

◄ # Batmobile (2012)

Although it features different details compared to the 2006 model, the 2012 Batmobile is still instantly recognizable as Batman's most famous and popular vehicle. It makes use of many LEGO elements that didn't exist back when the original model was designed, such as the vents on the sides, the angled exhaust pipes behind the canopy, and even the twin flames flickering in back.

DATA FILE

Set Name: Batmobile

Year: 2012

Set Number: 30161

Pieces: 45

Tinted canopy

Super-fast racing wheels

Bat-symbol hood sticker

Clear yellow headlights

MINI-MOBILE

Packaged in a bag as a promotional item, this micro-scale Batmobile is much too small to hold a minifigure driver. The model is built with a handful of carefully-selected elements, which cleverly replicate the sleek curves and smooth finish of much larger LEGO models.

BAT-VEHICLES

THE LEGO DC Super Heroes line features many models that are familiar for fans of the original LEGO Batman theme. But, just like the Dark Knight himself, they've all been completely redesigned for a totally new building and playing experience. With different sizes, details, and hidden surprises, these high-speed, high-tech vehicles are the latest tools in Batman's battle against crime!

▼ Batwing (2012)

Smaller and more nimble than its 2006 predecessor, the new Batwing retains the original's bat-symbol shape and the split-apart wings that conceal secret weapons. Only this time, the hidden weapons are a pair of blue-tipped flick-firing missiles designed to attack aerial threats, such as the Joker's own rebuilt Joker Copter.

Flexible tail-tip

Rear halves of wings are hinged to swing up

Bat-symbol decals

Under-wing flick-missiles

BRICK FACTS
The mini Batbomb's wings are made from a pair of LEGO minifigure weapon ax blades!

Black-costumed Batman

Wing lights

FRONT VIEW

BATBOMB
A hatch in back of the Batwing opens to reveal a button inside. Press it to drop a bat-winged mini seeker bomb!

BACK VIEW

DATA FILE

Set Name: Batwing Battle Over Gotham City
Year: 2012
Set Number: 6863
Pieces: 278

Adjustable handlebars

Exhaust pipes

Batcycle (I)

A well-equipped vigilante always has back-ups. In LEGO DC Super Heroes, Batman has his choice of two different Batcycles. This one, included in The Dynamic Duo Funhouse Escape set, matches Batman's blue and gray uniform and boasts sharp angles and finned exhaust pipes in back...

DATA FILE

Set Name: The Dynamic Duo Funhouse Escape
Year: 2012
Set Number: 6857
Pieces: 380

Both tires
the same size

Batcycle (II)

...while the more curved and streamlined Batcycle from the Batcave set has a darker color scheme, a pair of firing flick-missile launchers, and an aerodynamic shield over the front wheel to protect the engine.

DATA FILE

Set Name: The Batcave
Year: 2012
Set Number: 6860
Pieces: 690

Flick-missile

PURSUIT MODE
The Batwing's wings can be flattened down to create a streamlined shape for pursuit.

Smaller
front
tire

Headlights

DATA FILE

Set Name: Bat Jetski
Year: 2012
Set Number: 30160
Pieces: 40

Movable fins

Bat Jetski

Like the mini-Batmobile, this small boat for patrolling Gotham Harbor is a special bagged promotional set. Unlike that microscale model, though, the Bat Jetski is built to minifigure scale and even comes with a Batman minifigure with a newly updated cowl piece to pilot it.

Water
blasters

BATMAN™ AND The Joker IN BATTLE OVER GOTHAM

THE BATSIGNAL!

THE BATWING LAUNCHES INTO THE SKIES...

SWOOOOSH

POLICE CHANNELS ARE REPORTING AN EXPLOSION DOWNTOWN...

MEANWHILE, IN DOWNTOWN GOTHAM...

HEE HEE HEE! BOOM!

THOOOM!

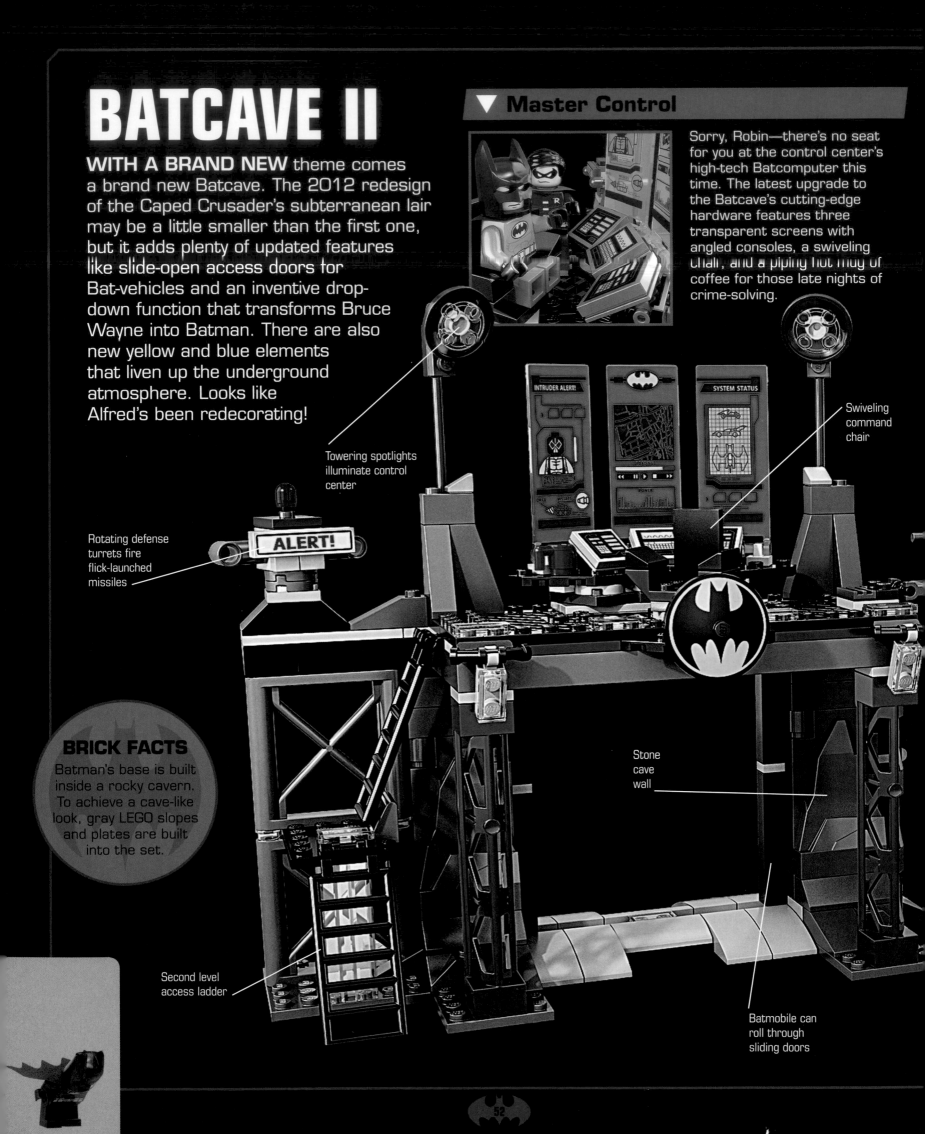

BATCAVE II

WITH A BRAND NEW theme comes a brand new Batcave. The 2012 redesign of the Caped Crusader's subterranean lair may be a little smaller than the first one, but it adds plenty of updated features like slide-open access doors for Bat-vehicles and an inventive drop-down function that transforms Bruce Wayne into Batman. There are also new yellow and blue elements that liven up the underground atmosphere. Looks like Alfred's been redecorating!

▼ Master Control

Sorry, Robin—there's no seat for you at the control center's high-tech Batcomputer this time. The latest upgrade to the Batcave's cutting-edge hardware features three transparent screens with angled consoles, a swiveling chair, and a piping hot mug of coffee for those late nights of crime-solving.

Rotating defense turrets fire flick-launched missiles

ALERT!

Towering spotlights illuminate control center

Swiveling command chair

INTRUDER ALERT!

SYSTEM STATUS

BRICK FACTS

Batman's base is built inside a rocky cavern. To achieve a cave-like look, gray LEGO slopes and plates are built into the set.

Stone cave wall

Second level access ladder

Batmobile can roll through sliding doors

DATA FILE

Set Name: The Batcave
Year: 2012
Set Number: 6860
Pieces: 689

▼ Bat-Gear

Next to the costume-change chamber is a brightly-colored storage rack for the Dark Knight's villain-battling gear, including two Batarangs, handcuffs (just the right size and shape to fit a minifigure's wrists), and a pair of binoculars. Batman keeps the tools of his trade handy and accessible—so he can grab them on his way to battle the bad guys!

POISON IVY (2012)

Poison Ivy is locked up tight in the Batcave's holding cell... at least until Bane breaks in to rescue her. Ivy's new minifigure is a lighter green than her 2006 version, with leaves printed on her red hair piece, a vine whip, and a new double-sided head.

Hotline phone to Commissioner Gordon

Secret hatch closes as Bruce Wayne drops down

Equipment storage wall

Guide-lights line dangerously high ledges

Fully-costumed Batman emerges at bottom

Energized holding-cell walls

DC HEROES & VILLAINS

THE LEGO DC Super Heroes theme opens up an entire world of LEGO construction beyond the borders of Gotham City. Finally, Batman can join forces with some of his most famous friends and teammates from the world of DC Comics, now captured in minifigure form for the very first time—and together they can battle a host of terrifying super-villains!

▼ Superman

Rocketed to Earth as a baby to escape his home planet's destruction, Kal-El gained incredible strength, flight, and vision powers. Now he lives a double life in the city of Metropolis as mild-mannered reporter Clark Kent and Superman, the world's most powerful super hero. His minifigure has two face prints: one serious and one with a cheeky grin.

Original hair piece with iconic S-curl

Symbol of Kryptonian heritage

Classic costume with red cape

▼ Wonder Woman

Diana is a warrior princess from the Amazon island of Themyscira. She uses her powers of super-strength, speed, agility, and flight to fight for peace and justice as Wonder Woman. In minifigure form, she has a unique hair piece with a painted tiara and her head piece features both smiling and battle-ready faces. Wonder Woman's magical Golden Lasso of Truth compels anyone it catches to speak only the truth. Made of flexible plastic, this accessory can fit around other minifigures to capture them.

Lasso of Truth

Unique hair piece with painted tiara

Elaborate costume print

BRICK FACTS
Superman was first available as a giveaway at New York Comic-Con in October 2011, with a card promoting the LEGO Super Heroes Unite! contest.

GREEN LANTERN
Based on his movie costume, this minifigure of Hal Jordan, the power ring-wielding hero Green Lantern, was exclusively released as a giveaway at San Diego Comic-Con and New York Comic-Con in 2011.

KRYPTONITE
Superman's greatest vulnerability is to Kryptonite, a glowing crystal created by the explosion of his home world of Krypton. In its most common green form, Kryptonite weakens Superman and removes his powers, which makes it highly prized by the bad guys. Other varieties like red and gold Kryptonite have additional strange and dangerous effects.

Translucent green LEGO crystal

LEX LUTHOR
Lex Luthor's brilliant mind is adept at both business and scientific invention, but his all-consuming hatred of Superman has made him devote all his genius mindpower to destroying the Man of Steel.

▼ Power Armor Lex

Seated at the controls of a mech (or piloted robotic armor) of his own design, Lex Luthor battles both Wonder Woman and Superman in this power-packed model. Ball-jointed limbs, a turning waist, and individually articulated fingers give Lex's power armor a high level of poseability. Translucent green elements make up its dangerous Kryptonite power source.

Kryptonite-powered weapon

Poseable fingers

Transparent power cable with green core

Heat-release vents

Click ball joints for strength

Wide feet for stability

KRYPTONITE GUN
Powered by a shard of raw Kryptonite in a transparent casing, Lex's cannon fires beams of strength-sapping radiation that can bring Superman to his knees— if they manage to hit him!

VIDEO GAME VILLAIN
In this special bagged pack given to people who pre-ordered the LEGO *Batman 2* video game, Luthor wears an armored battle suit and carries his Deconstructor weapon, which can break apart any structure made with black LEGO bricks in the game.

DATA FILE
Set Name: Superman vs. Power Armor Lex
Year: 2012
Set Number: 6862
Pieces: 207

THE JOKER

WHEN BATMAN returned for LEGO DC Universe Super Heroes, it was obvious that his arch-enemy couldn't be far behind. In fact, as the lone villain to make appearances in multiple sets in the first year of releases, the Joker is tied with Robin the Boy Wonder as the second most prolific minifigure in the theme—a fact that probably drives the Joker batty!

White ungloved hands

Larger acid-squirting flower

Remote control from set 6857

▶ The Joker (2012)

The Clown Prince of Crime is back, and he's just as mercilessly mirthful as ever. The new Joker retains his classic purple suit, but with the addition of a checkered green vest and lots of extra detail on the front and back of his torso. He sports a different hairstyle and has two new faces: a sarcastic smirk and his trademark toothy grin.

CRANKY CLOWN
The Joker is aided and abetted in his antisocial antics by a brand-new henchman who looks pretty grumpy despite his clown makeup. The Joker's name and face are printed on the back of his jacket.

THE JOKER

Custom "J" tailfin

Spinning rotor blades

◀ The Joker Copter (2012)

Along with the new Joker comes an all-new Joker Copter. This one has three rotor blades, a quartet of flick-firing missiles, and a Joker-faced "toxic laughing gas" bomb with a big orange clown nose that fires out the front when you slam a button in the back.
There's also a ladder for the Joker to hang off and wave his new prank gun around.

DATA FILE

Set Name: Batwing Battle Over Gotham City
Year: 2012
Set Number: 6863
Pieces: 278

Joker-face logo

Rope ladder

Laughing gas bomb

CATWOMAN

CATWOMAN STRIKES again! It may be six years later, but Gotham City's most talented cat burglar is still up to the same old tricks. Along with her Catcycle, Catwoman's second set includes a buildable Gotham street corner complete with mailbox, traffic light, newspaper stand, and a pile of boxes—perfect props for Batman to demolish with his Batarang as he tries to prevent Catwoman's speedy getaway.

DATA FILE
Set Name: Catwoman Catcycle City Chase
Year: 2012
Set Number: 6858
Pieces: 89

Stolen diamond

Headlight

▶ Catcycle (2012)

Catwoman's sleek new motorbike shares the basic construction and color scheme of the original LEGO model, but different details give it a slightly less cartoonish cat-like design. Gone are the obvious eyes and ears, and the back now looks like it has a long black tail with a brake-light at the end.

BRICK FACTS
Catwoman's mask may look like the same one she came with in 2006, but it's actually a new piece with closer-together eye holes!

Three-way traffic light

Mailbox

Whip storage clip

Flip-down bike stands

▼ Catwoman (2012)

Updated costume printing

Catwoman's second minifigure is based on the same costume as her first one, but with a completely new torso print. Her new design continues on the back of her torso and her old rope belt has been replaced with a new, trendier version.

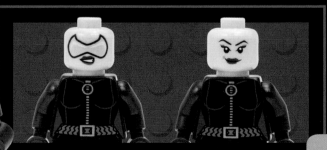

CAT'S FACE
Catwoman now wears purple lipstick, has blue goggles instead of silver, and bears a wicked expression on both of her faces.

▲ Gotham Street Corner

This section of Gotham City sidewalk isn't just for decoration. The traffic light at the top of the tall pole is held in place by a hook made from a minifigure wrench accessory, making it easy to knock down onto Catwoman's bike—or the Dark Knight's head if you'd prefer to let her escape with the loot this time!

Stolen bank safe

Articulated crane arm

TWO-FACE

TWO-FACE IS BACK, and that means twice the trouble for Batman and the good citizens of Gotham City. This villain may have a whole new style, but he is still of two minds about everything—including whether he should drive off with his boosted bank safe, or just blow it open on the spot!

Flick-fire missile launcher

DATA FILE

Set Name: Batmobile and the Two-Face Chase

Year: 2012

Set Number: 6864

Pieces: 531

Rotating cannon

New silver coin with printed decoration

▶ Two-Face (2012)

Harvey Dent has dropped his old look for an outfit based on his very first comic book appearance in 1942. Decked out in an orange and purple suit, with an updated face print, his 2012 minifigure really stands out from the crowd.

Reinforced prison-bar bumper

▲ Two-Face's Tow Truck

Two-Face's ride is just as divided as its owner. A combination of brightly-colored bricks and warning-stripe stickers decorate this beefed-up tow truck with a half-orange, half-purple theme—right down to the swiveling and jointed crane arm in back. In keeping with Two-Face's split personality, each side of the truck is armed with a different weapon.

HENCHMAN #1

HENCHMAN #2

DOUBLE TROUBLE
This time around, Two-Face has the help of a pair of henchmen in matching two-toned jackets. Although he often works with twins, these guys don't seem to be related.

Blast-out window

Teller booth

Opening door

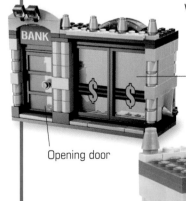

◀ Gotham City Bank

What's a bank robbery action scene without a bank? This bank section features a teller window and computer, a safe stuffed with hundred-dollar bills, and a big double-window that "explodes" out with the twist of a lever. The bank guard has a walkie-talkie and handcuffs… but will that be enough to stop Two-Face?

BANK GUARD 2012

BANE

IT LOOKS LIKE Bane hasn't forgotten his vendetta to break the Bat! Still as strong and ruthless as ever, he has discovered the secret location of the Batcave and burrowed his way in with the help of a powerful drill tank. The bundle of dynamite he's brought along can do a lot of damage—but once he's pumped up on Venom, Bane can probably wreck the place with his bare hands alone.

Light illuminates dark caves and tunnels

Flick-fire missiles

Exhaust vent

Drill spins when tank rolls

BRICK FACTS

This set doesn't include Bane's beloved childhood teddy Osito, but there is one in the LEGO® Minifigures line if you want to complete his gear!

DATA FILE

Set Name: The Batcave
Year: 2012
Set Number: 6860
Pieces: 689

Rubber treads

DYNAMITE

◀ Bane (2012)

Although Bane wears the same costume as in 2006 (and throughout his comic book appearances since his introduction in 1993), his minifigure now wears a black suit instead of blue. His mask and torso details have also been redesigned with a more prominent zipper on his forehead and a red buckle on his belt. He's got more defined muscles, and he's taken his gloves off, too—looks like he means business!

▲ Drill Tank

Built for smashing through cave walls and tunneling into underground lairs, Bane's drill tank is just as solid and tough as its driver. A LEGO® Technic gearing mechanism hidden inside makes the big silver drill in front spin when the tank drives forward (or backward) on its rubber treads, and a pair of flick-fire missiles deals with any walls or vehicles that get in the way.

BACK OF THE PACK
The printing on the reverse of Bane's torso has changed as well. His Venom dispenser tube now curves around more and plugs into the back of his mask at a single central point.

HE'S GAINING ON US!

SWOOOOSH

UH-OH...

BOOM

THUNK

END OF THE ROAD, TWO-FACE. YOU'RE GOING BACK TO JAIL.

UHHHH...

THE FUNHOUSE

WHY SHOULD BATMAN be the only one with a secret headquarters? The Joker and the Riddler have joined forces to build their own booby-trapped Funhouse to challenge the wits and reflexes of the Dynamic Duo, and they've even brought Harley Quinn along for the ride. Batman and Robin are about to discover that it's not all fun and games at this crazy carnival!

Cane is a crowbar piece

Rare purple hands

◀ The Riddler (2012)

The Joker may have a wild imagination, but the Riddler is definitely the brains behind the Funhouse. He has even installed a riddle-dispensing replica of his head to tease the heroes with tricky trivia. The Riddler's new minifigure has a redesigned, more muscular torso and a belt, a bowler hat, and a question-mark cane.

DATA FILE

Set Name: The Dynamic Duo Funhouse Escape
Year: 2012
Set Number: 6857
Pieces: 380

◀ In Jest

No one ever accused the Joker of being humble—his grinning face is plastered all over the Funhouse! It's not the only expression his 2012 minifigure is capable of, though. Flip his face around and it's a whole new look for the Dark Knight's laughing nemesis (see also p.56).

Coaster rails

Car smashes through Joker-face gate

Trivia booth, featuring a riddle-asking Riddler's head

▲ House of Fun

Each of the villains gets his or her own section of the Funhouse to play in. The Riddler has a hidden trap door, Harley Quinn has a rocking floor panel and a giant hammer to send Batman flying, and the Joker rules the heights with a remote-control crane to dangle the captured Teen Wonder over a barrel of toxic doom... and fish.

Sign tells everybody who's in charge

RIDDLE ME THIS
Pull out the LEGO Technic axle and the floor drops away in the Riddler's trap. As usual, he's left a clue for escaping: amongst the question-marks on his "Danger Ahead" sign is an arrow pointing out the danger!

Turn wheel to lower the rope

Hero-smacking hammer

Trick floor plate rocks from side to side

▼ **Harley Quinn (2012)**

The second version of Harley Quinn is similar to the first, but with an updated torso print featuring a pointier clown collar and two new expressions: a mischievous smirk and a smile to match Mister J's. Her runaway roller coaster car is part of a trap for Batman, but she's just as likely to ride it herself for fun.

Colors match Harley's costume

Translucent carnival lights

Barrel full of Joker Venom

Sinister staircase

BRICK FACTS
Most of the LEGO DC Universe Super Heroes models, including this one, come with a comic book telling that set's story!

LEGO® ULTRABUILD

TALLER THAN a minifigure! Quicker to build than a Batmobile! It's LEGO® Ultrabuild! Launched alongside the first series of LEGO DC Universe Super Heroes sets in 2012, these big, chunky "constraction" (a combination of construction and action) figures use a ball-joint assembly system and clip-on armor plates to make bigger, ultra-poseable, powered-up heroes and villains.

DATA FILE

Set Name: Batman
Year: 2012
Set Number: 4526
Pieces: 40

▼ The Joker

The wildly unpredictable Joker lives up to his reputation... who would have guessed his Ultrabuild figure would have more pieces than any character on this page? The Ultrabuild Joker may lack the broad shoulders of the good guys, but he makes up for it with his spiked power suit and translucent blaster.

Maniacal grin

"Shocking" electro-tie

Curved coat-tail spikes

Brightly-colored costume

DATA FILE

Set Name: The Joker
Year: 2012
Set Number: 4527
Pieces: 57

Non-removable mask

Soft plastic wing-spike

Bat-symbol chestplate

Fists with sculpted fingers

Bat-Sword splits apart

Protective armor

▲ Batman

Never one to be left behind by a new technology, the Dark Knight has upgraded his armor to face the Joker. Along with converting his cape into a set of spiky wings, he's replaced his usual Batarang with a giant double-bladed Bat-Sword. Each ball-joint on the Ultrabuild figures can hold many different positions, making the characters extremely poseable.

Green Lantern

The first non-Bat character to get an Ultrabuild set, Green Lantern is based on Hal Jordan's classic costume from the comics. Green Lantern's power ring lets him project constructs of solid energy, with their shapes defined by his imagination and the strength of his willpower. The set represents one of these constructs with a clear green spiked mace with a spinning tip.

DATA FILE
Set Name: Green Lantern
Year: 2012
Set Number: 4528
Pieces: 38

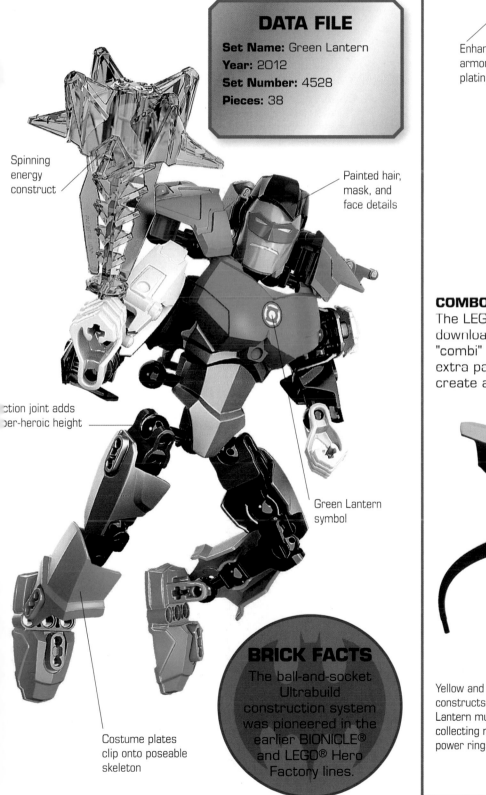

Spinning energy construct

Painted hair, mask, and face details

...ction joint adds ...er-heroic height

Green Lantern symbol

Costume plates clip onto poseable skeleton

BRICK FACTS
The ball-and-socket Ultrabuild construction system was pioneered in the earlier BIONICLE® and LEGO® Hero Factory lines.

Electricity-collecting antennas

Enhanced armor plating

Joker Venom spikes

Extra-purple pants

COMBOS
The LEGO DC Universe Super Heroes website features downloadable instructions for alternative builds and "combi" versions. These upgrade an Ultrabuild figure with extra parts taken from a second figure, which combine to create a more powerful version of the character.

Yellow and orange constructs—Green Lantern must be collecting more power rings!

Advanced Oan armor for extreme conditions

BEYOND THE BRICK

BEHIND THE mask of the Batman is the face of billionaire playboy Bruce Wayne. But what lies beyond the bricks of the LEGO® Batman™ and LEGO® DC Universe Super Heroes sets? On the following pages you'll find an exclusive look behind the scenes at the design and development of these action-packed themes, from hand-sculpted prototypes to the early concept versions that were refined and rebuilt into the final vehicles and locations of the LEGO DC Universe... plus some of the merchandise inspired by the models!

BEHIND THE SCENES

JOAKIM KØRNER Nielsen is Design Manager of the LEGO® Super Heroes design team in Billund, Denmark. He has worked at the LEGO Group for five and a half years, previously working as a Designer on the LEGO® Star Wars™, LEGO® Pirates of the Caribbean™, and LEGO® SpongeBob SquarePants™ themes. He has been involved with the LEGO DC Universe Super Heroes team since its conception. DK interviewed Joakim to discover the secrets behind how the super sets and minifigures are designed and made.

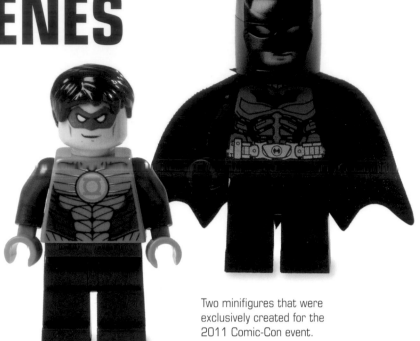

Two minifigures that were exclusively created for the 2011 Comic-Con event.

Who are the members of the LEGO Super Heroes design team, and what are their roles?

There are eight members of the team in total. As Design Manager I lead the design process and support the designers. We have four designers—Sven Robin Kahl, Marcos Bessa, Luis Castaneda, and John Cuppage—who build the actual models; Senior Designer Gitte Thorsen who hand sculpts new elements; and Graphic Designers Martin Fink and Thomas Ross Perry, who work on the decorations for bricks, sticker sheets, and minifigures. Many of us have previous experience of working on other licensed themes, such as LEGO® Star Wars™ or LEGO® Harry Potter™.

How do you research and find inspiration for new models and minifigures?

The initial concept phase can begin up to a year and a half before the launch of a set. We research the DC universe by reading the comic books and watching the relevant movies. We take inspiration from both classic comic content and newer materials—such as the new movies. When a new movie is coming out, we will read the script and visit the set to get inspiration for characters, vehicles, settings, and scenarios that we might want to design a set around. This can be invaluable for incorporating small details into the sets for fans. Then we will work very closely with DC.

From left: Sven Robin Kahl, Designer; Thomas Ross Parry, Junior Graphic Designer; Marcos Bessa, Designer; Gitte Thorsen, Senior Designer; John Cuppage, Designer; Martin Fink, Graphic Designer; Joakim Kørner Nielsen, Design Manager; Luis F. E. Castaneda, Designer

Can you tell us about how you work with DC Comics?

We are in constant ongoing dialogue with them. We will have suggestions about what we might want to create, and so will they—for example, what vehicles would we like to produce, and what would their functions be? LEGO Batman and Super Heroes sets are very much character based, so it is important to know a lot about the characters, and DC can give the overview and information that we need. When we have agreed on concepts we will send them 2D sketches of possible models, prototypes of minifigures, and have many development meetings, after which DC will give their official approval.

and play functions. It is important that functions are obvious enough. It's also crucial that the model or set is fun to build.

The Building Instructions team has to look at it from their point of view— we might need to change the color of a piece so that it will be clear in the building instructions. They know what kids can

"WHAT IS OF UTMOST IMPORTANCE FOR US IS THAT THE SETS ARE EXCITING FOR KIDS, SO WE TEST THE MODELS WITH CHILDREN AND LISTEN TO THEIR FEEDBACK."

Luis F. E. Castaneda sketching new concept directions that could be explored in bricks.

Early concept sketch by Luis F. E. Castaneda.

What is the design process for creating a LEGO Batman or LEGO DC Super Heroes set from start to finish?

After our dialogue with the partners we go deeper and begin to explore the model we are going to produce. We sketch ideas for features and functions. We evaluate whether we need any new elements like a wig for a minifigure, or a cockpit for a flying machine, and which stickers will be needed. We decide which elements we need and how to move forward. Then there are several processes we work through to get everything perfect.

What is of utmost importance for us is that the sets are exciting for kids, so we test the models with children and listen to their feedback. We also have to ensure that we are making the model or set the right quality and pitching it at the right price point. When we have the result of these tests, we put the model through the internal quality control process— known as the Model Review process. We test for stability

handle, what skills are involved. We test for quality and safety and any possible bad experiences— will it fall apart once built, for example. It has to work every time, even if the bricks aren't put together very well or if it has been played with many times.

The next step is to receive the final approval from the licensor. At this stage, the model will be finalized and locked into the system. After this, the process passes over to the team that creates the building instructions...

A sketch model for a small promotional model of the Batmobile.

BEHIND THE SCENES

How are the LEGO Super Heroes sets different from other LEGO sets?

A LEGO Batman set should always feature Batman doing battle against a villain. It should always be based on a really good story—one that kids can't wait to build and play. As a theme, and as the name suggests, LEGO DC Universe Super Heroes is all about the characters. It all starts with the super hero and the super-villain: Who are the heroes? What are they like? Who are they fighting? If you compare this to other LEGO themes—in LEGO® City, for example, the product might be a fire truck. Here, the product is the character. The DC universe is vast and exciting— it's not just about Batman. Now that we have added the Superman and Wonder Woman minifigures to the range, we have much more variety.

Hand sculpted element by Gitte Thorsen. A 3:1 model is sculpted by hand, scanned into a virtual version, and prepared for production at the correct scale.

A sketch model by Luis F. E. Castaneda. It was modified before appearing in the 6860 Batcave set.

Did you have to create any new LEGO elements for the theme?

The Batman and Super Heroes sets have allowed us to create lots of new LEGO elements—particularly for the minifigures. Lots of the comic book characters have iconic features—Superman's s-curl, Batman and Catwoman's cowls, and Two-Face's hairpiece, for example—have all been made into unique LEGO elements. We try to use existing pieces for buildings and vehicles if possible and keep the focus on the characters.

Which minifigure from the theme is your favorite?

Naturally, Batman looks cool in all his minifigure variations. He has a lot of gadgets and vehicles, which is great for LEGO play. But also Martin's design of the new Joker minifigure is so colorful—madness and silliness combined in one minifigure.

Which is your favorite set from the theme?

The Funhouse, which Sven built, is my favorite set so far. It has the right mix of LEGO humor and the right comic book feel, and has had good feedback from everyone!

A sketch model by Joakim Kørner Nielsen. An exploration into how to create Wonder Woman's Invisible Jet.

Were any sets or features particularly challenging to design?

Marcos designed the feature in the new Batcave where Bruce Wayne transforms into Batman. That's really cool. It's important to have the wow factor and an element of surprise to keep that feeling of newness. It's good to have something out of the ordinary. That was actually quite difficult and challenging to make as, of course, we only have LEGO elements to build from. We have to make sure all the functions still work—even if small children haven't pushed all the bricks together in the right way, and even after it's been played with lots of times.

> **"SOMETIMES WE MIGHT PUT A DESIGNER'S INITIALS, OR BIRTHDATE, OR SOMETHING ON A LEGO ELEMENT—SMALL DETAILS TO DELIGHT HARDCORE FANS."**

And were there any minifigures that were particularly challenging to create?

Wonder Woman was a challenging minifigure to make. We had to make sure she was true to her DC character. We had to design a new hairpiece, which was very complex. That was the hardest minifigure we worked on last year.

Are you a DC Comics fan?

With all the research we have to do (which is an excellent part of the job) it is hard not to get interested! I'm not a hard-core fan, but I do love Batman as a character, because he has no superpowers, but still beats all the bad guys, and has great weapons and gadgets. The Batmobile is really cool.

What would you do if you were Batman for the day?

I would probably drive the Batmobile and press all the buttons!
   But if I could be any DC Super Hero, it would have to be Superman, as he has the best superpowers (flying!), but looks like a normal, nice boy and lives a fairly normal life.

Sven Robin Kahl is designing one of the new elements for the theme with a 3D program.

As designers, do you get to hide any secrets or jokes within the sets?

Yes, but I don't want to give anything away! We do include small details that only hardcore fans would notice, like something written on a newspaper tile for example. Sometimes we might put a designer's initials, or birthdate, or something on a LEGO element—small details to delight hardcore fans. The fans like to talk about these kinds of things on the forums and try to find the initials of the designer, etc.

A sketch model by Marcos Bessa of a vehicle for Mr. Freeze.

Which character from the DC Comics universe would you most like to make into a LEGO minifigure?

There are lots of amazing DC characters that we would love to make into minifigures. The new LEGO Batman game gives you some examples. There are endless possibilities. The Flash is one example, as he has a cool helmet that could work well as a LEGO piece with the small wings.

Is there a location or vehicle you would love to make into a LEGO set?

As a child I used to love watching the Superman movies and I would love to see something like the icy Fortress of Solitude as a LEGO set.

A sketch model by Luis F. E. Castaneda where the humorous side of the super hero universe is explored.

If you could combine LEGO DC Super Heroes with any other LEGO theme, what would it be?

I think it would have to be the classic Space theme. Imagine aliens attacking Earth with the super heroes defending!

MERCHANDISE

THE WORLD OF LEGO Batman includes more than just construction sets. Along with two blockbuster video games and an animated TV mini-movie, you can show you're a fan with clothing, key chains, fast food toys, pens, posters, pillowcases, and even a *LEGO Batman: Secret Files and Origins* comic book given out at the San Diego Comic-Con in 2006. Here's just a sampling of all the merchandise out there!

BATMAN KEY CHAIN (2012)

Printed LEGO logo plate

BATMAN KEY CHAIN (2006)

Metal key ring

▼ Magnet Sets

Sold in packs of three, LEGO minifigure magnets are designed to stick to fridges and other metal surfaces. The ones manufactured for the original LEGO Batman line have magnets embedded inside their legs, while the new LEGO DC Universe Super Heroes sets consist of minifigures with magnetic 2x4 brick display stands.

Removable joke-gun accessory

Magnetic stand

Non-removable cape (head is permanently attached)

ROBIN KEY CHAIN (2006)

MAGNET SETS (2006)

THE JOKER MAGNET (2012)

▲ Key Chains

Who could be better at guarding your keys than Batman? The LEGO Extended Line division has released a dozen different key chains from the DC Universe, each equipped with a minifigure on a metal chain. Of course, choose a villain like Catwoman, Harley Quinn, or the Riddler, and there's no guarantee where your keys may end up…

BATCAVE COMIC BOOK (2012)

▲ Mini-Comics

LEGO Batman's adventures continue in the mini-comics that are included in most LEGO DC Universe Super Heroes boxes. With sound effects but no dialogue, they tell stories about the models and minifigures while showing off the set's buildable features and functions.

LEGO BATMAN CAP (2006)

Bat-symbol on brim

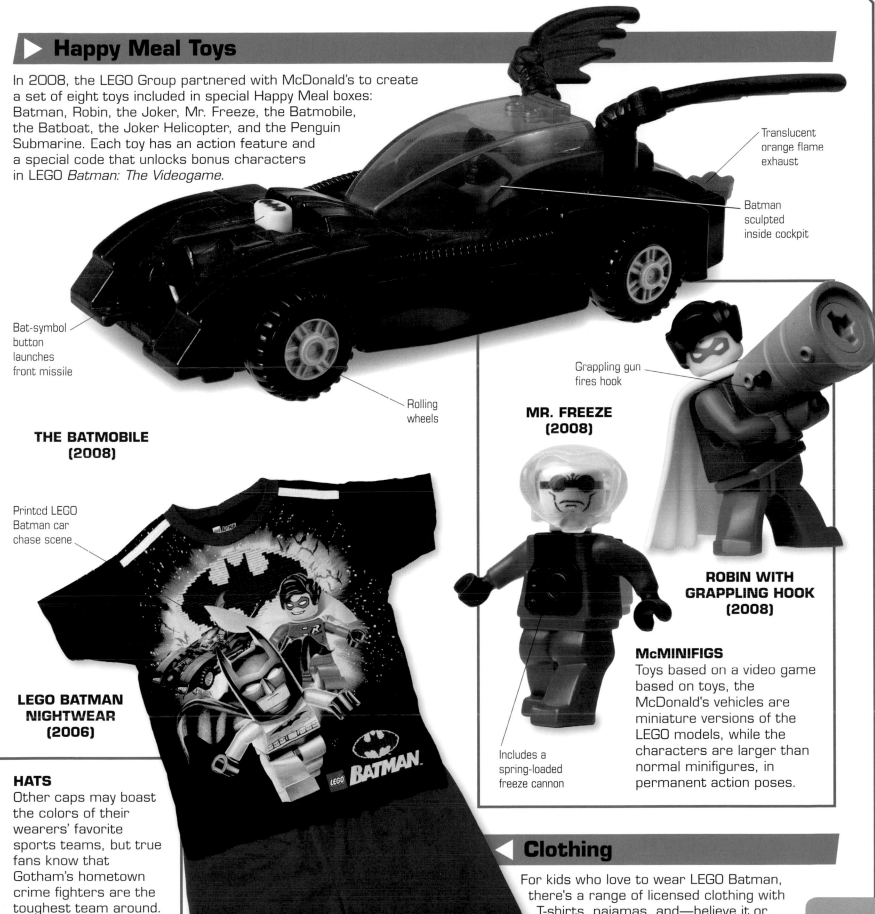

▶ Happy Meal Toys

In 2008, the LEGO Group partnered with McDonald's to create a set of eight toys included in special Happy Meal boxes: Batman, Robin, the Joker, Mr. Freeze, the Batmobile, the Batboat, the Joker Helicopter, and the Penguin Submarine. Each toy has an action feature and a special code that unlocks bonus characters in LEGO *Batman: The Videogame*.

Translucent orange flame exhaust

Batman sculpted inside cockpit

Bat-symbol button launches front missile

Rolling wheels

**THE BATMOBILE
(2008)**

Grappling gun fires hook

**MR. FREEZE
(2008)**

**ROBIN WITH
GRAPPLING HOOK
(2008)**

Printed LEGO Batman car chase scene

**LEGO BATMAN
NIGHTWEAR
(2006)**

Includes a spring-loaded freeze cannon

McMINIFIGS
Toys based on a video game based on toys, the McDonald's vehicles are miniature versions of the LEGO models, while the characters are larger than normal minifigures, in permanent action poses.

HATS
Other caps may boast the colors of their wearers' favorite sports teams, but true fans know that Gotham's hometown crime fighters are the toughest team around. Several different LEGO Batman hat designs have been produced since 2006.

◀ Clothing

For kids who love to wear LEGO Batman, there's a range of licensed clothing with T-shirts, pajamas, and—believe it or not—underwear decorated with minifigure designs of the Dynamic Duo and their fearsome foes. There's even apparel for adult fans who are still young at heart!

GOING DIGITAL

WHEN YOU'VE already brought justice to the world of plastic bricks, what's a Dark Knight to do for an encore? Why, take the action into the digital world, of course! LEGO® *Batman™: The Videogame* lets players control Batman and his sidekicks on a swinging, climbing, punching, and building mission all across Gotham City, battling a legion of the Caped Crusader's greatest foes. Or you can turn the tables and play as the villains in their sinister scheme to take over the city. And that's just the start of LEGO® Batman's video game adventures...

INTRODUCTION

When LEGO® Batman™: The Videogame arrived in late 2008, mania for the movie *The Dark Knight* was in full swing. The game offered a welcome, family-friendly way to play in the world of the Caped Crusader, mixing hero vs. villain action with engaging puzzles and LEGO bricks. And best of all, if your character fell to pieces, it would pop right back together again!

▲ The Video Game

Following a scene-setting rooftop battle, the game starts with a bang as Batman's enemies stage a mass escape from Arkham Asylum. Play begins in Story Mode, but once a player successfully completes a level, it's unlocked in Free Play mode with access to extra characters and secret areas.

▶ Concept Art

The artists at TT Games kicked things off by creating a series of concept sketches to help define the look of Gotham City in the game. They chose to design a realistic city-scape instead of one made entirely out of LEGO bricks, so that when players did encounter bricks during a level, they would know that they could build something with them. Colored paintings then fleshed out the sketches and created different moods for the various locations where Batman and his allies would have to go as the game's original story unfolded.

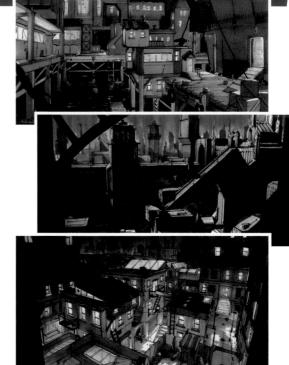

◀ Vehicles

Some levels of the game can't be traversed on foot. That's when players get to use their game controllers to take command of Batman's most iconic vehicles. It's an armament-packed armada that looks just like the LEGO sets the in-game designs are based on—except that these models can really drive, fly, and cruise their way through the digital streets, skies, and waterways of Gotham City. The villains have vehicles too, and the fun really starts once you enter Free Play mode!

▶ LEGO® CITY in Gotham

What do you do when you need to fill a busy city with cars, trucks, and flying machines that aren't driven by Batman and company? Fortunately, the game designers had a whole extra city to draw on—LEGO® CITY, that is! Thanks to special guest stars from the long-running classic LEGO theme, Gotham's police force is equipped with 2008's mobile Police Command Center and other crime-stopping vehicles.

▼ Interactive Environment

Gotham City's environment is far from static. Game characters can fire grappling lines to climb up buildings, walk on tightropes to get across gaps that are too far to jump, and assemble items out of LEGO bricks to solve puzzles... or smash them to pieces! Don't forget to explore everywhere you can possibly go, because you never know where you might find more LEGO studs to collect and turn in for special bonuses.

▲ Video Sequences

In addition to the introduction that shows the break-out by all of Gotham City's bad guys, the progress of the game's story is revealed through fully animated video sequences that take place between levels. Keep a close eye on the action, because there are jokes and visual gags sprinkled all throughout the animations.

THE HEROES

NO HERO SHOULD have to fight alone. That's why Batman has a team of highly-trained sidekicks to help him take down Gotham City's toughest crooks. In LEGO *Batman: The Videogame*, Batman, Robin, Batgirl, and Nightwing each have special suits that give them unique abilities and upgrades for solving puzzles, surviving traps, and defeating all of the escaped villains!

DEMOLITION SUIT
Switching to this costume lets the Dark Knight drop and detonate explosives.

GLIDE SUIT
This winged costume allows Batman to jump over gaps and glide down to the ground.

SONIC SUIT
This costume's sonic blaster fires a beam that vibrates glass bricks until they shatter.

▼ Batman

In his standard appearance in the game, Batman wears his gray and black costume from the 2006 LEGO Batman theme. He uses his Batarang for blocking bullets and long-distance attacks, and his grapple ability for scaling Gotham's tall buildings. He can use a Suit Swapper device to change his look, and find special bricks to upgrade his suits' powers.

Black and gray costume from 2006 LEGO sets

Digital minifigures are a lot more flexible than plastic ones!

▼ Batgirl

The lack of a real minifigure isn't enough to keep crime fighter Barbara Gordon out of the LEGO Batman game! As Batgirl, she can wear all of the same costumes as Batman.

Game-only mask piece

Cape is yellow in the final game

BRUCE WAYNE
Even Batman's billionaire-playboy civilian identity can fight in the game—by swinging his ever-present briefcase!

Robin

In the LEGO *Batman* game, Robin carries a yellow and green Batarang of his very own. Like Batman, the Boy Wonder can use Suit Swappers to change into different costumes that give him new skills and abilities, or use them on their own in Free Play mode.

2006-style hair piece

Tim Drake's original Robin costume

TECHNOLOGY SUIT
This high-tech outfit lets Robin hack into computer panels and control mechanical items.

ATTRACT SUIT
With this suit on, Robin can vacuum up red, yellow, and green bricks and build new objects out of them.

MAGNET SUIT
With the help of magnets on his feet, Robin can walk straight up metal walls and ceilings.

WATER SUIT
Thanks to its flippers and air supply, this costume lets Robin explore deep underwater.

Everyday Heroes

You don't need superpowers to make a difference. Along with unlockable characters like the Huntress and Nightwing's secret identity Dick Grayson, here are some of the other good guys in the game.

ALFRED
Serving tray in hand, Bruce Wayne's butler can be unlocked as a playable character for Free Play mode.

COMMISSIONER GORDON
The chief of the GCPD arrests captured crooks and is a boss when you play on the villain side.

SECURITY GUARD
Security guards, military police, and other nameless good guys are always ready to defend Gotham City from attack.

Nightwing

A bonus character who can be purchased once you've collected 125,000 LEGO studs in the game, Nightwing uses his circus training to fight and walk quickly on tightropes. Since he's the original Robin, he also has access to all of the Boy Wonder's special costumes and upgrades.

Same spiky hair piece as his LEGO minifigure

Wields Escrima sticks and custom Batarangs

THE VILLAINS

ARKHAM ASYLUM'S ESCAPED criminals have divided into three groups, led by the Joker, the Riddler, and the Penguin, each with its own fiendish goals. After beating one of the three story chapters as the heroes, you can play it again from the villains' point of view and try to conquer Gotham City yourself.

2006 minifigure design

▼ The Riddler

The puzzle-loving Riddler doesn't care about chaos or revenge—he just wants loot, and plenty of it! That's why he's plotting to break into the Gotham Bullion Fortress and steal the city's gold, leaving Batman clues along the way. He has an alternate suit and hat in the DS version of the game.

Cane controls weak-willed minds

▶ The Joker

The Joker leads Harley Quinn, the Scarecrow, Killer Moth, and the Mad Hatter on a mission to engulf Gotham City in laughing gas. In battle, he carries machine guns and uses an electrified joy-buzzer for surprise attacks.

TROPICAL JOKER
The Joker sports an unlockable tropical costume, complete with Hawaiian shirt.

CLOWN GOON
A Joker henchman dressed as a silent-but-deadly mime.

▼ The Penguin

As one of the three main baddies behind the breakout, the Penguin leads his gang of Bane, Killer Croc, Man-Bat, and Catwoman in a plot to use his penguin minions to take over Gotham. He can use his trick umbrella as both a weapon and a gliding device.

Hat unleashes penguin bombers

Fiendish formal wear

▼ Catwoman

A member of the Penguin's team of villains, Catwoman can use her acrobatic double-jump ability to get the edge on her opponents. Her classic purple costume from the comics is available as an alternate outfit, and her alter ego Selina Kyle appears in the DS version.

Slashes enemies with claws

▼ Mr. Freeze

FREEZE RAY

Mr. Freeze's freeze gun traps his enemies in blocks of ice, leaving them vulnerable to shattering single-hit strikes. If left alone too long, the ice will break and free his victims.

As a member of the Riddler's team, Mr. Freeze pays a visit to his old hideout in an ice cream factory to retrieve his freeze cannon. When he sticks around to thaw out his frozen Freeze Girl underlings, he gives the Dynamic Duo a chance to show up and put him back on ice.

Freeze gun freezes certain liquids

Climate-controlled suit enhances strength

▶ Bane

Along with a Venom-fueled immunity to toxins, Bane's greatest asset is his unstoppable physical might, with which he can even out-arm-wrestle Killer Croc! Smarter than he looks, Bane should probably know better than to rely on the slippery Penguin as a partner-in-crime.

Knee disables opponents

▼ Poison Ivy

Poison Ivy uses her fast-growing mutated plants and her green-skinned vegetable goons to aid the Riddler's team. Her natural immunity to poison gas and toxic waste makes her perfect for infiltrating hazardous environments. The DS version of the game also includes her Pamela Isley identity and an alternate costume.

Poison kiss

Athletic skills

LETHAL LIPS

Not only can Poison Ivy jump higher than most characters and get through doors that only female villains can access, but her poisonous pollen kiss is deadly, both at a distance and up-close and personal.

▶ Harley Quinn

Whose team would Harley be on but the Joker's? As the criminal clown's chief assistant, the ex-psychiatrist helps him capture Commissioner Gordon and set up his laughing gas attack on Gotham City. She can also be found in her Dr. Harleen Quinzel guise in the game's DS version.

Early version of her game model

MORE VILLAINS

THE MASTERMINDS behind the Arkham break-out know exactly what kind of heroics Batman and his team are capable of. That's why they've recruited every super-villain in Gotham City—not to mention hundreds of goons, henchmen, and bodyguards—to join them in their scheme to tear the city down and rebuild it in their own crooked image!

◀ Two-Face

Two-Face uses his armored truck to rescue the Riddler from Batman and Robin, and helps him steal a laser cannon from Wayne Enterprises. Constantly flipping his coin, he uses twin revolvers in his attacks... of course!

▼ ...and the Rest

And the villains don't end there. The ranks of Batman's Rogues Gallery are boosted by extra characters from the comics like the DS-exclusive Firefly, Black Mask, Hugo Strange, Mr. Zsasz, Talia al Ghūl, the Ventriloquist, and Scarface... not to mention these fearsome familiar faces!

MAD HATTER
Wonderland-obsessed Jervis Tetch can leap into the air with the propeller in his gigantic hat.

KILLER MOTH
He thinks he's the anti-Batman, but most people just see this colorful crook as a joke.

KILLER CROC
Croc's amphibious abilities are especially useful for a sewer-based prison break-in.

CLAYFACE
With his shape-changing powers, Clayface can transform his limbs into various powerful weapons.

HUSH
This bandage-wrapped villain is one of Batman's most mysterious and dangerous foes.

RĀ'S AL GHŪL
The centuries-old "Demon's Head" is a bonus character who is unlocked when you've collected all of the mini-kits in the game.

MAN-BAT
Mutated scientist Dr. Kirk Langstrom blocks Batman's path to the Penguin at the Gotham Zoo.

SCARECROW
The Scarecrow flies to the Joker's assistance by engaging the Batwing in a daring aerial duel.

82

THE VEHICLES

AS BATMAN AND his team battle their way through a Gotham City overrun by weapon-packing crooks and escaped super-villains, they rely on Batman's high-tech vehicles—like the Batwing, the Bat-Tank, and the Batboat—to help them succeed in some of their biggest missions. Unfortunately for the heroes, the bad guys have brought along a few colorfully dangerous vehicles of their own!

▼ Bat-vehicles

As Batman's primary form of transportation, the fast, armored Batmobile is equipped with a tow-cable to help it drag other vehicles. Piloted by Robin, the Batcopter carries bombs that can destroy silver LEGO bricks. And whilst Bruce Wayne's private jet may not have weapons, its speed provides a real boost in Free Play mode.

▼ Villains' Vehicles

Many of the bad guys in the game have their own custom vehicles, from the Riddler's quick and deadly question-mark jet to the Joker's ice cream truck, Mr. Freeze's cold-blasting iceberg, and the Mad Hatter's glider and steam boat, which isn't very fast, but is great for crashing into things.

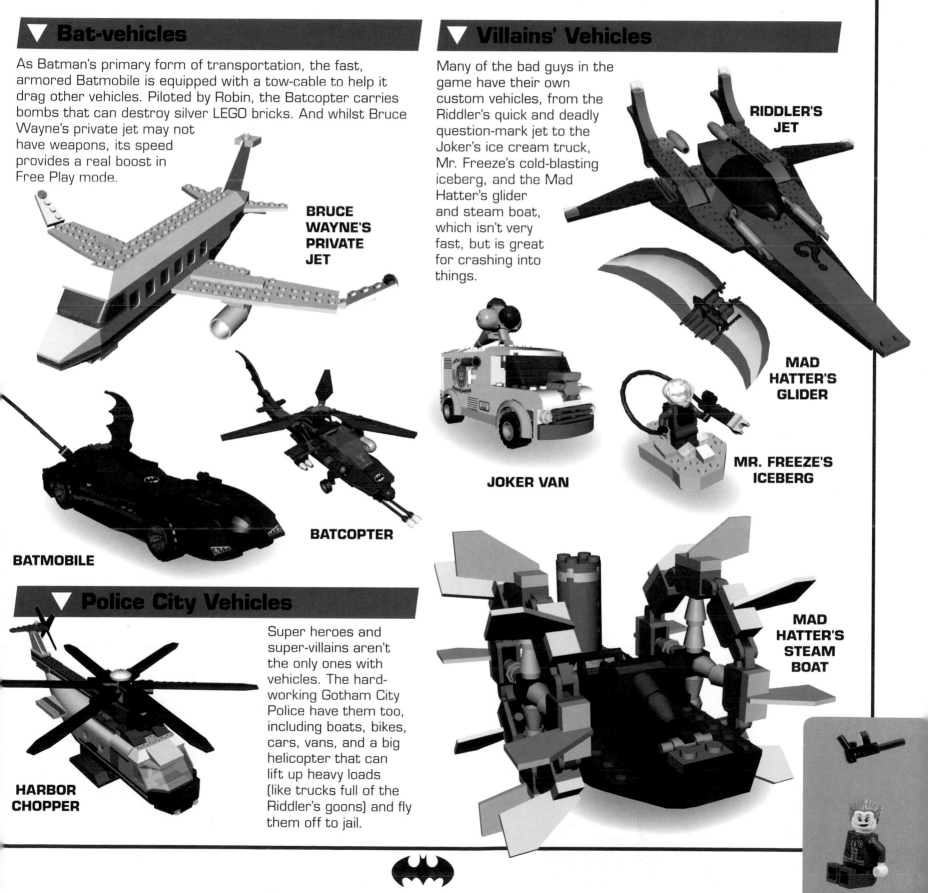

BRUCE WAYNE'S PRIVATE JET

BATMOBILE

BATCOPTER

RIDDLER'S JET

MAD HATTER'S GLIDER

JOKER VAN

MR. FREEZE'S ICEBERG

MAD HATTER'S STEAM BOAT

▼ Police City Vehicles

Super heroes and super-villains aren't the only ones with vehicles. The hard-working Gotham City Police have them too, including boats, bikes, cars, vans, and a big helicopter that can lift up heavy loads (like trucks full of the Riddler's goons) and fly them off to jail.

HARBOR CHOPPER

THE LOCATIONS

GOTHAM CITY isn't an easy place to live in, but with so many super-villains and henchmen running amok, the Gotham City of LEGO *Batman: The Videogame* has never been more dangerous. It will take all of the Caped Crusader's skills to survive these lethal locales—especially if the boss villains waiting there have anything to say about it!

▼ Botanic Gardens

Here in Gotham's Botanic Gardens, you can grow giant carrots, build a tractor out of bricks, and find Batman's Sonic Suit, which you'll need to get rid of a glass door and other objects blocking your way. Robin's Attract Suit will help you make a giant plant to use as a jump-boosting trampoline.

▲ Arkham Asylum

Gotham City's bad guys all break out of Arkham Asylum at the beginning of the game, but there must be no place like home, because the high-security hospital also serves as the game's hub when you play through the story from their side. You'll find a Character Customizer and a trophy room here, too.

STREETS OF GOTHAM
In one fast-paced level of the game, the Joker joins forces with Killer Moth in a race to reach the sanctuary of the cathedral. Try to avoid getting captured by the Gotham City police if you can!

▼ The Ice Cream Factory

Mr. Freeze and the Riddler team up to invade the factory in search of the freeze cannon.

This abandoned facility for making tasty frozen treats used to be Mr. Freeze's sub-zero lair. Now he's paid a return visit to pick up an old invention. You'll need to switch ice cream cone colors, commandeer a cold-blasting cannon, and make good use of Robin's Magnet Suit to beat this one.

▶ Police Headquarters

An imposing edifice that only features in animated cut-scenes, this is the home of the Gotham City Police Department and Batman's trusted friend Commissioner Gordon. On its rooftop sits the Bat-signal, which the Commissioner lights to summon the Dark Knight in times of trouble—like this one!

Gotham's finest, hard at work… or are they goofing off now that Batman's in town to clean things up?

Separated by obstacles, the villains need to take turns solving puzzles to help each other through the level.

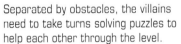

In Free Play mode, you can explore the carnival as any character you've unlocked so far.

◀ The Funfair

The Joker and Harley Quinn have lured good old Commissioner Gordon to this freaky fairground, and it's up to the Dynamic Duo to save him. Along the way, they'll have to climb ladders, slide down slides, and battle the acrobatically adept Harley to a standstill.

AERIAL VIEW

These images are overhead views of the levels "Little Fun at the Big Top" and "Batboat Battle." Bet Batman would love to have maps like these!

▶ Gotham Cathedral

Don't forget to stop and take in the sights of Gotham's world-famous architecture.

Time for the ultimate challenge: keeping the Joker from unleashing a laughing gas attack on Gotham City. Build a water cannon out of bricks, scale a towering cathedral and take down the Joker's helicopter to stop the Clown Prince of Crime's mischief once and for all—or at least until the sequel!

LEGO® BATMAN™ 2

IT'S GOOD TO have friends. With the world even bigger, the villains even tougher, and the stakes even higher in LEGO *Batman 2: DC Super Heroes*, it definitely comes in handy for the Caped Crusader to be able to call in some extra superpowered support from his famous teammates in the Justice League!

▼ Batman

Digital Batarang

Batman makes an eagerly-awaited return in LEGO *Batman 2: DC Super Heroes*, teaming up with his fellow heroes. He dons a whole new set of powered-up costumes on his quest to save not just Gotham, but the entire LEGO DC world from the schemes of Lex Luthor and the Joker.

Black costume from 2012 LEGO sets

▲ 2012 Game

With the worldwide success (more than 11 million copies sold) of the first LEGO Batman video game, it was no surprise that the LEGO Group and TT Games teamed up to make a sequel based on the 2012 LEGO DC Universe Super Heroes theme. LEGO *Batman 2* features new suits, new gadgets, new vehicles, new powers... and, for the first time, voices for its minifigure characters!

SENSOR SUIT
Batman's new Sensor Suit lets him look through walls and activate Stealth Mode to turn invisible.

POWER SUIT
This amped-up armor lets Batman pull super-strength handles and fire sticky bombs to destroy silver bricks.

ELECTRO SUIT
This costume insulates Batman against electrical traps and lets him control their power.

► Superman

With his incredible strength, near-invulnerability, super-breath, and ability to fly, you'd think Superman could take care of any problem on his own. But thanks to Lex Luthor's Kryptonite-charged weaponry, not even the Man of Steel can tackle this crisis alone—though he and Batman are not too happy to be working together at first.

Nothing messes up this guy's hair!

Details straight from the minifigure

SUPER-VISION
The Last Son of Krypton brings plenty of special skills to the table in LEGO *Batman 2: DC Super Heroes*. One of the most useful may be the heat vision beams he can fire from his eyes, which can be used to destroy gold bricks to reveal hidden items or puzzles trapped inside.

▼ Wonder Woman

LEGO *Batman 2* sees the digital debut of Wonder Woman in LEGO minifigure form. In the game, she can lend Batman a helping hand with her own super-strength and other powers, not to mention rounding up crooks with her famous golden lasso.

Game model has many more facial expressions than the minifigure

Charge into action with the Lasso of Truth

▼ Lex Luthor

Luthor kicks off the events of LEGO *Batman 2* by breaking the Joker out of jail and offering him a deal: if the Clown Prince of Crime will help Lex get his hands on some Kryptonite, he'll share the power of his black-brick-disassembling Deconstructor weapon.

The Deconstructor

Kryptonite powers most of Luthor's tech

▼ Green Lantern

Green Lantern can use his power ring to transform green LEGO bricks into constructs to solve puzzles. He can also fly and fire ring-charged blasts at enemies, making him a key part of the final battle to defend Gotham City.

Emblem of the Green Lantern Corps

▼ The Flash

The Flash is the DC Universe's most well-known super-speedster. He is also known as The Fastest Man Alive. LEGO *Batman 2* features current Flash Barry Allen who works in a crime lab. He can run as fast as Gotham's fastest cars, and build quicker than any of the other characters.

Lightning-themed costume details

CATHEDRAL

What could be making the cathedral's tower bell ring? Batman can't rely on Batarangs to save the day this time, so look for help from somebody with heat vision who isn't afraid of heights.

NEW DESTINATIONS

THE DECONSTRUCTOR gives Lex Luthor and the Joker the power to do more than just dismantle Batman's favorite toys! They plan to use it to change the face of Gotham City itself. In LEGO *Batman 2: DC Super Heroes*, you'll visit both familiar and new locations, including Wayne Tower, the Town Hall, the Observatory, the Theater, and the Yacht Club—and other exotic and brick-filled travel spots!

▼ Ace Chemicals

The Dark Knight returns to where it all began at this famous chemical plant, where a fall into a vat of toxic goo first gave the Joker his green hair and sunny disposition. Drop on in—just not literally!

BOTANIC GARDENS

This overgrown greenhouse is now the lair of the beautiful-but-deadly Poison Ivy. You'll find her perched on her Venus Flytrap throne, but don't forget to look for trapped citizens as you battle your way through her botanical booby-traps.

▼ Gotham Funland

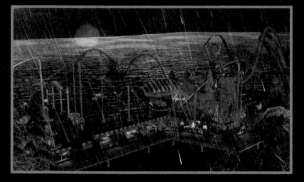

At the Gotham Funland amusement park, you can take a ride on a roller coaster and play plenty of fun mini-games, though you'll need to have the right suits to complete them. Collect two red bricks to unlock special vehicles.

▼ Park

Set in the center of Gotham City, the park is big and full of collectable items. You can play a battleship mini-game on the pond, solve the maze, and find a pair of helicopters parked on top of the surrounding buildings.

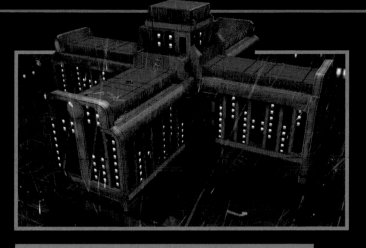

BRICK FACTS
Scattered around Gotham City's locations are hidden Gold Bricks. There are over 250 of them to find in total!

▲ Gotham General

One of Gotham City's iconic buildings is its general hospital, where the doctors and nurses are used to treating the victims of laughing gas attacks, giant mallets, and the occasional robot penguin attack. You'll find Hush waiting up above—appropriate, since the guy used to be a doctor.

POLICE STATION
With three giant statues permanently on guard, you wouldn't think the Gotham Police Station would have much worth stealing, but that doesn't keep the sneaky Catwoman away from its rooftop!

▼ Wayne Manor

Located on the island north of the city, the traditional home of the Wayne family hides not one secret, but two. Fly over the mansion and look down, and you'll see that it's built in the shape of a bat. And of course if you venture beneath, you'll find...

◄ The Batcave

...Batman's secret headquarters, the hub for the game's heroes. Here, you can use the game's Character Customizer to make your own super hero, or access the Batcomputer for story levels, free-play levels, and the all-important Gotham City map. You can even hop in any unlocked vehicle and go for a race.

MAKING THE DIGITAL WORLD

JONATHAN SMITH IS Head of Production at TT Games Publishing. It's his job to make sure that TT is making the right games, at the right time, in the right way, and he has lately been busy working on the new LEGO® Batman™ video game! DK interviewed Jonathan to discover how the games are made.

How did you react when you found out that you were going to be making a new LEGO Batman video game?

We had such a brilliant time making the original game back in 2008, and we always knew we'd come back to the DC Universe at some point. When we got confirmation that the LEGO Group had a new range of DC Super Heroes minifigures and sets to launch in 2012, that seemed the perfect time to do it. Everyone immediately had loads of ideas.

Who was involved in making LEGO *Batman 2*?

We've had over 150 people working on LEGO *Batman 2*, and I wish there was space to name them all! The LEGO *Batman 2* storyline was originated by our Creative Director Jon Burton, and the script was written by David A. Goodman. John Hodskinson was the Game Director, and David Hoye was the Lead Artist; he worked closely with our Head of Art Leon Warren and concept artist Tim Webster to create the visual expression of Gotham City and all our game levels. Cutscenes and characters were animated under the supervision of Jez Pardon, our Head of Animation.

What did you do to prepare for making the game?

Any new game development begins with a phase of research—and when we're lucky enough to be allowed to play in these amazing worlds, that's a hugely enjoyable process.

The streets of Gotham City glow in LEGO *Batman 2*

Comics from all decades, and the various animated series are our primary reference sources. We're given brilliant advice by the folks at DC and Warner Bros. And we get to see all the LEGO sets during development—including prototypes that they don't take to the final stages.

What goes into making a LEGO Batman video game?

Because we've been making LEGO games for many years now, there are lots principles that everyone on the team follows instinctively, to make the foundation a fun LEGO experience. We have consistency of team and technology, a proven and regularly updated LEGO parts library from which to build new models, and we stick to fundamental rules like: "everything made of LEGO bricks should be interactive and fun to play with." We match the new LEGO models and characters precisely; we ensure we have the rights we need to use authentic music, and on that solid foundation we build as much crazy new stuff we can think of!

Both the LEGO Group and DC Comics have been fantastically supportive during development of LEGO *Batman 2*. We have a very close relationship with the LEGO Group, built up over many years, and DC are full of ideas and suggestions for characters or abilities

Giant LEGO statues in Gotham City

that would make the game more fun. We're always learning new things. Damian Wayne, for example, is an important new character. He didn't exist when we made the first game, but he's now available as a purchasable extra in some versions of LEGO *Batman 2*.

Finally, we have a big group of very talented testers who work on our LEGO games. We couldn't finish our games without them—they're all so dedicated, hard working, and accomplished at pinning down every detailed problem.

How did you make this game different from the first one?

We're proud of what we achieved with the first game, but that was many years ago. This new game is full of new technology and features. Our new lighting and physics systems make the game world look more realistic and rich; there are new characters with brand new abilities. And there are two massive new areas that are completely unique. LEGO Gotham City is brought to life as our biggest-ever playable environment, full of secrets and action. Flying over the rooftops as Superman, then landing and switching to Batman, calling in the Batmobile, and cruising down the streets, is an experience not to be missed! On top of that, we're telling a totally original story, in a totally new way. LEGO *Batman 2* will be the first LEGO game to have "talking" minifigs!

What's the objective of the latest game?

Gotham's greatest super-villain, the Joker, has teamed up with Superman's nemesis Lex Luthor, and their masterplan will wreak havoc not just on Gotham but ultimately on the whole world! It's up to you to stop them. Initially you'll be in control of the Dynamic Duo—Batman and Robin— but it will soon become apparent that the task is too daunting even for them. You'll be joined by Superman, and ultimately the entire Justice League! It's full of action and showcases all the coolest heroes in the DC Universe, with unique LEGO humor!

Robin has ace acrobatic skills

How did you design the characters that don't yet exist in LEGO minifigure form?

With many years of experience, our LEGO character artists are experts at the creation of new LEGO characters for our games. They carefully analyze reference images of the required characters, then extract the key visual elements, distill, refine, and express them through the unique LEGO visual language.

One of the great things about DC Universe characters is the fact that they all look so distinctive, with instantly memorable moves and personalities... so much of the creative work has already been done for us in all the decades these characters have already lived—on page and on screen.

Lex Luthor and the Joker make a terrifying team

Were there any highlights for you in creating this game?

The work of the design, programming, and animation teams combined to create the experience of Superman flying through LEGO Gotham City is definitely one of the greatest achievements of LEGO *Batman 2*. I personally enjoyed writing the lines for Vicki Vale, the newsreader who appears before each level, and the actor who plays her, Anna Vocino, delivered them with real comic panache.

Which characters from the game are your favorites?

My personal favorite hero is Robin. Often overlooked, he has a bunch of incredibly useful, fun, and unique abilities—including acrobatic skills, his Ice Suit, and the mighty Hazard Cannon. Favorite villain: Lex Luthor. He's always got a plan!

All of the members of the Justice League are great characters to play as—not only because they're intrinsically cool personalities, with distinctive looks, but because they've each got a wide array of different powers and abilities. Cyborg, for example, is not only super-strong, but also has the ability to shoot a laser beam from his eye, and move metal objects from a distance using electro-magnetic powers.

Batman and Superman are forced to team up as part of the story. It's an uncomfortable match to begin with, but eventually they'll need to work effectively together in order to deal with the villainous threat of Lex Luthor and the Joker. Now there's another great team...

What's your favorite Bat-vehicle or Bat-gear?

The Batmobile is incredibly fun to control, with powerful weapons. Batman has plenty of gadgets to see him through the game's challenges. The Power Suit is one of the best—it not only gives him extra strength and some cool new fighting moves, but actually fires missiles. And Batman just looks so cool as he stomps around in it!

Can you tell us about your favorite battles and levels?

There is a sequence of spectacular face-offs. The battle against the Joker's giant robot as it falls from Wayne Tower is a particular highlight. Everyone loves exploring Gotham City, but my personal favorite level is set in Metropolis, home of Superman and Lex Luthor. When our heroes visit Lexcorp—Luthor's offices and research facility—not only is it stylish and full of cool tech, but Lex is such a show-off that he's made the entire building itself constantly rotate! There's even an entire secret level, if you're able to discover it...

The JL team up with Batman and Robin in the latest game

MINIFIGURES

THE BASIC LEGO® minifigure arrives for the builder to assemble in three sections: a head; a torso and arms; and a waist and legs. Extra detail is added with hair elements, printed decoration, and special accessories— and few minifigures are as colorful, detailed, and geared-up as the smaller-than-life heroes and villains of the LEGO® Batman™ and LEGO DC Universe Super Heroes themes!

BATMAN (2006)
Sets: 7781, 7783, 7785

BATMAN (2006)
Sets: 7779, 7780, 7782

Every Batman minifigure includes a removable mask with a minifigure face printed underneath. Batman's white eyes are created by a headband above the minifigure's normal black-dot eyes.

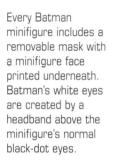

BATMAN (2007)
Sets: 7786, 7787

BATMAN (2008)
Sets: 7884, 7886, 7888

BATMAN (2012)
Sets: 6857, 6858, 6860

BRUCE WAYNE (2006)
Set: 7783

BRUCE WAYNE (2012)
Set: 6860

NIGHTWING (2006)
Set: 7785

ROBIN (2006)
Set: 7783

ROBIN (2008)
Set: 7885

ROBIN (2012)
Sets: 6857, 6860

BATMAN (2012)
Sets: 6863, 6864, 30160

ALFRED (2006)
Set: 7783

SUPERMAN (2012)
Set: 6862

WONDER WOMAN (2012)
Set: 6862

LEX LUTHOR (2012)
Set: 6862

THE JOKER (2006)
Sets: 7782, 7888

THE JOKER (2012)
Sets: 6857, 6863

CATWOMAN (2006)
Set: 7779

CATWOMAN (2012)
Set: 6858

POISON IVY (2006)
Set: 7785

POISON IVY (2012)
Set: 6860

SCARECROW (2006)
Sets: 7785, 7786

HARLEY QUINN (2008)
Set: 7886

HARLEY QUINN (2012)
Set: 6857

TWO-FACE (2006)
Set: 7781

TWO-FACE (2012)
Set: 6864

BANE (2007)
Set: 7787

BANE (2012)
Set: 6860

THE PENGUIN (2006)
Sets: 7783, 7885

PENGUIN MINION (2006)
Sets: 7783, 7885

KILLER CROC (2006)
Set: 7780

MR. FREEZE (2006)
Sets: 7783, 7884

THE RIDDLER (2006)
Sets: 7785, 7787

THE RIDDLER (2012)
Set: 6857

THE JOKER'S HENCHMAN (2006)
Sets: 7782, 7888

THE JOKER'S HENCHMAN (2012)
Set: 6863

TWO-FACE'S HENCHMAN (2006)
Set: 7781

TWO-FACE'S HENCHMAN (2012)
Set: 6864

TWO-FACE'S HENCHMAN (2012)
Set: 6864

MR. FREEZE'S HENCHMAN (2006)
Set: 7783

ARKHAM GUARD (2006)
Set: 7785

ARKHAM GUARD (2006)
Set: 7785

BANK GUARD (2012)
Set: 6864

INDEX

Main entries are highlighted in bold. Sets are listed by their full name.

NEW YORK, LONDON, MELBOURNE,
MUNICH, AND DELHI

Project Editor Victoria Taylor

Editorial Assistant Emma Grange

Senior Designer Lisa Sodeau

Designer Jon Hall

Additional Designers Lisa Robb
and Anne Sharples

Managing Art Editor Ron Stobbart

Publishing Manager Catherine Saunders

Art Director Lisa Lanzarini

Publisher Simon Beecroft

Publishing Director Alex Allan

Senior Production Editor Jennifer Murray

Senior Production Controller Melanie Mikellides

Photography by Andy Crawford, Daniel Lipkowitz,
Tina Nielsen, and Gary Ombler

First published in the United States in 2012
by DK Publishing
375 Hudson Street
New York, New York 10014

12 13 14 15 10 9 8 7 6 5 4 3 2 1
001—183102—Sep/12

Page design copyright © 2012 Dorling Kindersley Limited

Color reproduction by Media Development Printing Ltd, UK
Printed and bound in China by Leo Paper Products

Acknowledgments
The publisher would like to thank Benjamin
Harper from Warner Bros. Consumer Products;
Corinna Van Delden, Randi Sørensen, Michael
Sørensen, and Joakim Kørner Nielsen at the LEGO
Group; Sam Delaney, Matt Ellison, Phillip Ring, and
Jonathan Smith at TT Games for supplying invaluable
images and information about the video game; Daniel
Lipkowitz for his research and writing; Andy Crawford,
Gary Ombler, and Tina Nielsen
for their photography; Shari
Last and Jo Casey for editorial
support; and Satvir Sihota for
design support.

2006 black and
gray Batsuit

LEGO chains hold
Batman captive

The Joker's
characteristic
manic grin

Discover more at
www.dk.com
www.LEGO.com
www.warnerbros.com